M000222111

A BOOK FOR

FAMILY

WORSHIP

A BOOK FOR

FAMILY

WORSHIP

Jim Cromarty

 EVANGELICAL PRESS

EVANGELICAL PRESS
12 Wooler Street, Darlington, Co. Durham, DL1 1RQ, England

© Evangelical Press 1996

All rights reserved. No part of this publication may be reproduced, stored in a retrieval system or transmitted, in any form, or by any means, electronic, mechanical, photocopying, recording or otherwise, without the prior permission of the publishers.

First published 1996

British Library Cataloguing in Publication Data available

ISBN 0 85234 388 4

The passages for meditation at the end of each chapter are from the Holy Bible, New International Version. Copyright © 1973, 1978, 1984, International Bible Society. Used by permission of Hodder & Stoughton, a member of the Hodder Headline Group. All rights reserved.

Other Scripture quotations in this publication are from the Holy Bible, New King James Version. Copyright © 1984 by Thomas Nelson Inc. All rights reserved.

Graphics in this publication on page 16, 19, 25, 27, 28, 40, 42, 45, 55, 58, 64, 70, 84, 91, 93, 96, 106, 109, 112, 113, 127, 130, 133, 142 (top) and 164 are used by kind permission of:

New Horizons Educational Computing Services
P.O. Box 658 Armidale
NSW 2350
Australia

Those on pages 37, 51, 57, 61, 76, 88, 94, 119, 134, 136 and 142 (bottom) are used by kind permission of:

Zedcor Inc. Permissions Department
3420 N. Dodge Blvd Suite Z
Tucson AZ 85712-5205
Australia

Other graphics in this publication are used under a Freehand licence in accordance with the T/Maker Company ClickArt Licence Agreement, Clipart Copyright @ 1984-1995 T/Maker Company.

Printed and bound in Great Britain at the Bath Press, Bath.

This book is dedicated
to
my mum

Contents

Preface

Family worship has a twofold aim. The primary aim of all worship, including family devotions, is to glorify God. Secondly, family worship is a means of instructing children in the knowledge of God.

We live in an age where the worship of God is largely ignored by all, and of those who attend worship, only a few are sincere followers of Christ. Knowledge of the Scriptures is lacking and few take seriously the truths of heaven and hell and Christ as being the only way of salvation.

Mention sin and hell and the world throws up its hands in horror. How dare Christians damage self-esteem by speaking of sin? And hell — this is thought to be a doctrine of the dark ages! But the truths of Scripture remain the same for all generations.

As parents we must face the grim reality that there is such a thing as 'original sin' and our children are all born into this world as sinners. David stated this truth when he wrote, 'Behold, I was brought forth in iniquity, and in sin my mother conceived me' (Psalm 51:5). Jesus confirmed it when he said, 'That which is born of the flesh is flesh...' (John 3:6). Yes, the human heart is corrupt! (Mark 7:21-23). Our children are born sinners and will die sinners unless a gracious God delivers them from sin's dominion. As Jesus told Nicodemus, so he says to all sinners who would be members of the kingdom of God: 'Most assuredly, I say to you, unless one is born again, he cannot see the kingdom of God' (John 3:3).

To so many these are fighting words. The old lie of Satan, of salvation by doing good works, is loved by the world. And how many Christian parents have been guilty of saying to their unconverted children, 'Be a good boy or girl and God will love you'?

Parents have a responsibility to train their children in God's ways. Our children are God's gift to us. In Psalm 127:3 we read, 'Behold, children are a heritage from the LORD...'

The greatest tragedy of all is to die unconverted. The destiny of all such sinners is hell — eternal punishment! The world may recoil in horror from these words, but they remain true.

Our greatest gift to our children is to teach them about God and their need of faith in Christ as the way of salvation. They must be taught that sin is a reality that can only be forgiven by a gracious God through his Son, the Lord Jesus Christ.

May people be able to say of you and your family what was said of Cornelius: 'There is a person who fears God with all his household' (Acts 10:2).

Christian parents must stand firm for God and his salvation in this age of 'live-as-you-like', materialism and the continual seeking after pleasure. I would encourage all parents daily to gather your children and worship God as a family. Teach your children the truths of God and continue to pray for their conversion. And make sure you set them an example of godly living. This book is aimed at helping parents in the great task of teaching their children about the wonderful works of God and salvation in Jesus Christ. May God be pleased to bless your endeavours.

Jim Cromarty
November 1996

1.   Never give up!

'Then his wife said to him, "... Curse God and die!"' (Job 2:9).

| **Read** Job 1:13 - 2:10 |

There are times in our lives when things go terribly wrong and we feel like giving up. Sometimes people are very ill and find that no treatment seems to help them. They often then feel like giving up living. They would rather be dead.

My brother and I used to spend a lot of time fishing. If we had no bites after several hours we would give up and go home. There is little value in wasting time.

I have a little dog whom I have called Wags, because he wags his tail continually. He is a Maltese and looks like a fluffy white ball. I have been training him to sit, stay and shake hands. My wife has been training him to leave the clothes and shoes alone. Sometimes I think he is learning very well, but there have been times when it all seemed a waste of time and we wondered if we should give up.

Sometimes in our Christian lives the going gets difficult. I am sure that many Christians have sometimes felt that remaining faithful to Jesus is so difficult that they could give up and go back to the world and their old way of life. But we should be very thankful that once God has begun the work of salvation in a soul, he will faithfully continue with that work until the saint reaches heaven (Philippians 1:6). God never gives up on his people!

I'm sure that when you finished today's reading about Job and all his troubles you wondered what kept him faithful to God. Job had lost his children, his farm animals and his servants. It must have broken his heart when he heard the bad news. But Job still loved God. He knew that the good things of life came from God and that God had the right to take away what he had given. Think hard about Job's words that follow:

> Naked I came from my mother's womb,
> And naked shall I return there.
> The LORD gave, and the LORD has taken away;
> Blessed be the name of the LORD

(Job 1:21).

Job knew that one day all his possessions would be left behind. He would die and could take nothing with him in death.

Then we read that Job was covered in boils. This must have been so very painful. When Job's wife saw him she told him to 'curse God and die'. What a terrible thing to say! Of course Job did no such thing. He loved God with all his heart and soul. Even though we later read of Job becoming downcast, he still remained faithful to God. In fact we read his great words of trust in his God: 'Though he slay me, yet will I trust him' (Job 13:15).

Job had trusted himself to God in both life and death. No matter what happened, he would continue to trust God. This is a real saving faith and is the faith that you need if you are to be saved. God only does what is best for us, to make us faithful Christians. Then he gets all the glory for his gracious work of salvation.

NEVER NEVER NEVER GIVE UP

Now every Christian finds at times that the going gets hard and when this happens he or she may think, 'What's the use? I can't go on any further! I'll give up!' Maybe the believer begins to give up reading the Bible and doesn't spend time in prayer. Sometimes the troubled Christian even gives up going to church for a time. There may be a time when he begins to believe that God doesn't care about him any more.

What, then, is the answer to this problem in the Christian life? The answer is so simple, yet so difficult. It is to remain faithful to God no matter what. When you don't feel like reading your Bible, then force yourself to read it. When you don't feel like praying, then pray on. When you don't feel like going to worship, force yourself to go.

King David tells us in Psalm 42 that there was a time when he was very 'cast down' (v. 5). His enemies were attacking him. He was forced to escape from Jerusalem. He longed to get back with his people to worship God with them. In fact we read David's question: 'I will say to God my Rock, "Why have you forgotten me?"' (v. 9).

David was very downcast. What was the answer to his problem? It was simple, but I'm sure he found it difficult. In the midst of all his problems David could write, 'Hope in God; for I shall yet praise him' (v. 11).

God has promised that he will never leave nor forsake anyone who loves Jesus (Hebrews 13:5). So when you feel like giving up your faith in Christ and going back to your sins remember that God loves you and will complete the work he has begun in your life.

Your godless friends might seem to be enjoying life much more than you. But don't let them lead you astray. Don't give up! Pick up your Bible and read and pray. Pray that the Holy Spirit might thrill your soul with the good news that your sins are blotted out and that you are on your way to heaven. Read about the glorious things that are in store for you when you reach heaven. Read about God's great love towards you. Just pray that God will keep you faithful and don't ever give up!

Discuss

1. Job's wife told him to 'curse God and die'. If he had cursed God, how might he have expected to die? (See Leviticus 24:13-16).
2. Talk about the things that make you happy and unhappy.
3. Why do you go to worship? Is this the right reason?
4. Have you ever felt like giving up attending worship? Why?

Meditate

Why are you downcast, O my soul?
Why so disturbed within me?
Put your hope in God,
for I will yet praise him,
my Saviour and my God
(Psalm 42:11).

Pray

1. If you are not a Christian pray that God might give you a saving faith in Jesus Christ.
2. If you are a Christian pray that you may be kept a faithful servant of Jesus.
3. Pray that the Holy Spirit might give you all an understanding of God's Word.
4. Sincerely ask God that every member of your family might know Jesus Christ as Lord and Saviour.

2. A Chinese puzzle

'Fathers, do not provoke your children to wrath, but bring them up in the training and admonition of the Lord' (Ephesians 6:4).

Read Psalm 34:8-14

Many people who read the Bible believe that its teachings are only for adults. They think the Bible has nothing really to say to children. But of course this is not true. Every word found in the Bible is there for all, young and old, to read and obey.

And the young people who are reading this book know that you must learn a lot of things while you are growing up. While you are at school you are taught to read and write as well as a host of other subjects. You learn sporting skills. And of course you learn how to get on with other people — how to be a good citizen of the country in which you live. There are some very difficult lessons you must learn and sometimes you will find problems that really test the brain.

I once found a Chinese wooden cube in a shop. When I got it home the piece of paper in the plastic covering told me that the cube consisted of a lot of small interlocking wooden blocks. That was all that was written.

So I set to work pushing here and there till finally I was able to move a block of wood. I made a sketch of what I was doing so I would be able to put the blocks back together again. After a day or two I was able to pull the block apart and put it together again.

My daughters, who had been watching and advising me what I should do, then took over and before very long they too could unlock the blocks and put them together again. So proficient did we become with the Chinese puzzle that we could pull the block apart with our eyes closed. But we couldn't put it together unless we watched what we were doing. There were no instructions with the puzzle but that made it all the more intriguing.

The Bible is God's instructions to all of us — both young people and adults. In fact there are special instructions given to parents concerning their children, as well as teachings directed to children and young people.

15

In Psalm 34:11 David wrote, 'Come, you children, listen to me; I will teach you the fear of the LORD.'

The most wonderful event that can take place in anyone's life is the new birth. That is when the Holy Spirit enters and changes a sinner's heart. He or she is given a saving faith in Jesus and so begins the Christian life. But children must be taught about God and the way of salvation.

The Chinese puzzle I bought had no instructions telling me how the block could be undone or put together again. It was just a case of 'keep trying'. But you have God's Word which tells you everything you need to know about yourself and the way of salvation.

King David thought so much of children that he wanted them to listen to him as he taught them about God. In Christian families parents want their children to grow up to be lovers and followers of Jesus Christ. So they will say to you young people, 'Come, you children, listen to me; I will teach you the fear of the LORD.'

Your mum and dad will want you to learn about yourself — to know that you are a sinner because you have broken God's law. They will want you to know about the gracious saving work of the Lord Jesus Christ. They will pray for you that God might bless you. They will take you to Sunday School and church so that you might learn more of God. And they will pray that one day you will say, 'I want Jesus to be my Saviour because I am a sinner and I can't save myself.'

When I was young I had my own Bible — I still have that Bible — and I read it. I didn't understand all that I read, but I read on. I can still remember my mum reading *Pilgrim's Progress* to my brother John and me. I can remember crying about some of the sad events that took place as Christian walked the pathway to heaven. I can still remember how happy I was when Christian finally crossed over the river and reached heaven, the Celestial City.

My brother John and I were greatly blessed in that we had parents and grandparents who were concerned about us — not only that we had food and clothes, but that we learned about the true God.

Parents who are reading these words, you have a great responsibility towards your children. You must teach your children the ways of God and not hand that responsibility over to others. It is your responsibility! Others can only assist you in your God-given task.

My little dog Wags is being taught to behave himself. He pays attention and over the months ahead I hope he will learn to obey. May all the readers of this book truly learn the ways of God and faithfully follow Jesus.

Discuss

1. What can your parents do to teach you the ways of God?
2. What did Nicodemus learn from Christ? (John 5:3,7).
3. What is a Christian?
4. Find a children's version of *Pilgrim's Progress* and start reading.

Meditate

He decreed statutes for Jacob
   and established the law in Israel,
which he commanded our forefathers
   to teach their children,
so that the next generation would know them,
   even the children yet to be born,
   and they in turn would tell their children.
Then they would put their trust in God
   and would not forget his deeds
   but would keep his commands
                       (Psalm 78:5-7).

Pray

1. Pray for parents as they carry out their God-given obligations concerning their children.
2. Pray for your minister and Sunday School teachers that they might teach you God's truth.
3. Ask God to give you an understanding mind as you read the Bible passages and each chapter in this book.

3. Do you like oysters?

'Oh, taste and see that the LORD is good; blessed is the man who trusts in him!' (Psalm 34:8).

Read John 1:35-51

God gave us taste buds so we could enjoy the great variety of foods found throughout the world. I enjoy Kentucky Fried Chicken as well as Chinese foods. I just love the taste!

For as long as I can remember my brother and I have always had a special liking for oysters. Some of our relatives used to catch them and every now and again a bag of oysters would be delivered to us on the farm. Our grandfather loved the taste of oysters and I'm told that John and I would sit beside him with our mouths wide open as he scooped the flesh out of its shell. Then in turn he would give each of us an oyster to eat.

The salty taste of the oyster is delicious. You have to taste one in order to appreciate its flavour. My wife doesn't like oysters. She says they look terrible. That means there is always more for me to enjoy. But I was certain that my daughters would cultivate a taste for those delicious oysters. I bought some and just as I was about to give them their first taste Valerie said, 'Oh, Jim, don't give them oysters to eat. They're terrible!' So none of my daughters eats oysters. They wouldn't even taste to find out if they liked them or not.

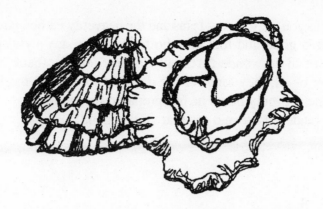

The only way to find out what a food is like is to taste it and see. The only way to find out if a person is worthwhile knowing is to 'taste and see' — go and speak to the person and learn about him or her.

Our Bible text invites us all to get to know God and discover his goodness. You will never really know God if you don't open your Bible and read about him. You must pray that God's Holy Spirit will make his home in your heart. Discover all that the Bible has to say about God's Son, Jesus Christ. The closer you get to him, the better you will know him.

Our reading is about the early days of Jesus' ministry. We find questions being asked by some who were interested in becoming disciples of Christ: 'Who is this Jesus?' And we find the answer given: 'Come and see!' These men would never know Jesus until they went to him and spoke to him. They needed to get close to Jesus in order to discover his character and his claims. They 'tasted' Jesus and saw that he 'was good'. Then they followed him.

Now Jesus has said to all people: 'Come to me, all you who labour and are heavy laden, and I will give you rest. Take my yoke upon you and learn from me, for I am gentle and lowly in heart, and you will find rest for your souls. For my yoke is easy and my burden is light' (Matthew 11:28-30).

There are many people who mock Jesus and make fun of Christians. In some parts of the world Christ and his followers are hated so much that they are killed. But people who do these terrible things have never 'tasted and seen' what the Lord is like. They have no personal experience of Jesus as the loving God who came into the world to save sinners. These people hate the good news concerning Christ and salvation.

Now what about you? Do you poke fun at people who are Christians? If you do it is because you do not know Jesus.

Christians are people who have seen their own sins and then come to know Jesus as Lord and Saviour. In order to know Jesus you must read your Bible and pray that God will show you what the Scripture is saying about his Son. You need to mix with Christians to hear what they are saying about the Jesus whom they love and who loves them.

19

Then as you get to know Jesus and the heavenly Father, you will discover that God is good and that all who trust in him are joyful people. Why? Because of all the wonderful things God has done for them. They are saved. And, best of all, they long for the day when they will meet Jesus face to face in the heavenly home he has prepared for them.

'Oh,' reader, 'taste and see that God is good!'

Discuss

1. What is an oyster?
2. How can you taste the goodness of God?
3. In our reading we met two of the apostles of Christ. Can you name all twelve? (See Matthew 10:2-4).

Meditate

Taste and see that the LORD is good;
　　blessed is the man who takes refuge in him.
Fear the LORD, you his saints,
　　for those who fear him lack nothing
　　　　　　　　　　　　　　　　(Psalm 34:8-9).

Pray

1. Pray that the Holy Spirit might give you a better understanding of Jesus Christ as Lord and Saviour.
2. Pray for the work of any missionaries you know.
3. Pray that God will give you courage to tell others about Jesus and what he has done for you and your family.

4.   A black bird

'Casting all your care upon him,
for he cares for you' (1 Peter 5:7).

Read Matthew 10:27-31

At any time of the year Australia has a great range of weather conditions. In one part of the country there can be bush fires, in another area the countryside can be flooded and then again somewhere else the people may be shivering in the cold. Australia is a very large island with a varying climate.

A pastor friend of mine lives in a cold part of the country. In fact it is so cold that even during the summer, fires are sometimes needed for warmth.

Recently Ted and his wife were to have some time away from their home. It was a cool day and they were unsure whether or not they should light the fire, leaving it to smoulder all day, so that the house would be warm when they returned. After some discussion they decided they wanted a warm home when they returned the next afternoon.

Now Ted had experienced a fire in the chimney. This happened when the soot which coated the inside of the fireplace caught alight. Flames would shoot out of the chimney on the roof and the sound of the air rushing through the fireplace and up the chimney sounded like a train racing through the house. So Ted decided that before he lit the fire he would clean the soot out of the lower part of the chimney. There was a steel sheet in the chimney holding a pile of soot so Ted knelt down and carefully began to drag it out.

As the pile of soot began to appear Ted got the fright of his life. Suddenly from the pile of soot something black darted at him. He fell back in shock as a frightened, soot-covered sparrow flew for the open door. Looking at his once white shirt, Ted saw patches of black ash everywhere. But the sparrow was free!

Had Ted lit the fire without cleaning away the soot the little sparrow would have remained trapped and been burned to death. Had the family simply gone away for several days without lighting the fire, the small bird would probably have died from thirst and the cold.

The sparrow could do nothing but sit in the soot and shiver. But God knew of its danger. Our reading tells us that God knows all that is happening in the universe — even the activities of the little sparrows.

In Australia nobody is really interested in a sparrow. They are small birds that hop about looking for food. They don't hurt anybody, but they are not as colourful as the parrots. People keep parrots and other colourful birds as pets, but I have never met anyone who had a pet sparrow. Isn't it wonderful to read in the Scripture passage that God is concerned about the well-being of all creatures, even the little sparrows? Not even a small sparrow falls to the ground without God's permission.

In fact we also read that God knows the number of hairs on our heads. I read somewhere that there are about 140,000 hairs on a normal head. There are less on mine as many have fallen out over the years! But God has kept an account of what has happened to every hair from my head.

But more wonderful still is the text for today. Peter tells us that God is concerned about people. In fact he urges all who are suffering to humble themselves and cast their cares upon himself. And why should they do this? Peter gives us the answer and it is truly amazing: 'He [God] cares for you!' The almighty God who created all things and by his power keeps the world functioning cares for sinful people. God's eye is upon you.

God's love is seen all around us. So many people have food to eat and homes in which to live. God even makes provision for those who hate him and want nothing to do with Jesus Christ.

We also read in Scripture encouraging words that speak to all of us who love God and his Son Jesus Christ: 'And we know that all things work together for good to those who love God, to those who are the called according to his purpose' (Romans 8:28). God cares for his people in a special way. Everything that happens in this world is for the good of Christ's followers and for the glory of God.

God saved each one of his people. He sent his Son Jesus Christ into the world to live a life of perfect righteousness and die bearing the penalty for their sin. All this Jesus willingly did for his people. And God is preparing a glorious and eternal home for all of them. May you be among those who have a place in heaven where Christ lives and reigns!

Remember, God cares for the little sparrows, so why should we be afraid of the events of this world? Jesus tells us, 'Do not fear therefore; you are of more value than many sparrows' (Luke 12:7).

Discuss

1. How can you cast your cares on God? (See Philippians 4:6-7).
2. Why do you think people are so precious to God?
3. How did God show the world that humans were precious to him? (See Romans 5:8; 8:32-39).

Meditate

How lovely is your dwelling-place,
   O LORD Almighty!...
Even the sparrow has found a home...
   where she may have her young—
a place near your altar,
   O LORD Almighty, my King and my God.
Blessed are those who dwell in your house;
   they are ever praising you

                  (Psalm 84:1,3-4).

Pray

1. Thank God for providing for your needs.
2. Praise God for his interest in you and your family.
3. Ask God to forgive your sins for the sake of Jesus who died upon the cross.

5. Safety in a tree — a saving God

'The LORD will be a shelter for his people' (Joel 3:16).

Read Acts 16:25-34

I love walking amongst the trees. In Australia we have the stately gum trees growing very tall. The smell of the eucalyptus is found everywhere. Trees are very valuable as material to build homes, construct fences, make furniture and so many other important things we need to make life easier.

Growing in our garden are many small shrubs that have a lot of flowers at various times of the year. When the flowers are in full bloom the birds have a great time sipping the sweet nectar. I even planted two trees just the right distance apart so that one day I could hang my hammock between them. But I think it will be quite a long time before the trees are strong enough to support me.

Cats enjoy the tree life and seem to love climbing amongst the branches for exercise. One day I saw a dog chasing our cat. He just ran for the tree and climbed up the trunk to a branch. He was quite safe there.

Lately I have noticed many birds making good use of the trees. Where I live we seem to have a lot of summer storms. We see the ominous dark clouds rising over the horizon and before long the rumble of thunder can be heard.

When a storm is on the way, I make sure the car is in the garage as I don't want hail damaging the paintwork. My wife makes sure the windows in our house are closed as she doesn't want a wet floor. When Wags hears the thunder he heads for the door and comes inside. He doesn't like the noise and must feel more secure lying on the floor between my feet.

But the birds flying around outside also sense that a storm is on the way. As it approaches, with lightning and thunder all around, I often see the birds flying about looking for a place of safety. And that is when the trees are very useful. There is safety for the birds when they land on the branches of the tree and hide from the wind and rain in amongst the leaves. I have

seen birds huddling together as the wind howled around the leaves and branches. They were safe. Sometimes leaves were broken off the tree, but still the birds were safe. And when the storm was over, out they would come knowing that it was safe to fly about in the open sky.

We all need a place of safety. I pray that your home may be a true place of safety for you. In my home I feel safe from what is happening in the world outside.

But remember that as sinners we are under God's anger, unless we have Jesus Christ as our Saviour. There is a day coming when the world will experience the storm of God's anger. The Bible tells us that such a day is coming — the day when Jesus Christ returns. The prophet Joel spoke of this day when he wrote:

The LORD also will roar from Zion,
And utter his voice from Jerusalem;
The heavens and earth will shake

(Joel 3:16).

How can you be protected from God's anger? The answer is found in our text and in today's reading: 'The LORD will be a shelter for his people.' 'Believe on the Lord Jesus Christ, and you will be saved...' Just as the birds found their safety from the storm by hiding themselves in the tree, so also sinners can find safety if they hide themselves in Jesus Christ. This means that sinners must go to Jesus, confess their sins and then trust themselves to him completely for safety from God's anger towards sinners.

Jesus has already suffered the storm of God's anger when he came to this world and died upon the cross at Calvary. So all who trust in him are safe. He has suffered in their place.

Always remember the Philippian jailer, who was told that by believing in Jesus he would be saved. He then trusted himself to Jesus and he is now safe for ever from the anger of God. In fact God loves him for the sake of Jesus, his beloved Son.

It is my sincere hope that you also are loved by God because you have trusted in Jesus Christ for salvation.

Discuss

1. What is meant by 'believing on the Lord Jesus Christ'?
2. How does Peter suggest we live, since Christ is to return? (See 2 Peter 3:11-14).
3. When will the great judgement day of God be?
4. How can you prepare for that day?

Meditate

God is our refuge and strength,
    an ever-present help in trouble.
Therefore we will not fear, though the earth give way
    and the mountains fall into the heart of the sea...
                                    (Psalm 46:1-2).

Pray

1. Pray for the coming again of the Lord Jesus Christ.
2. Thank God for sending Jesus Christ into the world to save sinners.
3. If you have not already done so, ask God to give you a saving faith in Jesus Christ.

6. Beware of the rock — an angry God!

'The stone which the builders rejected has become the chief cornerstone... And whoever falls on this stone will be broken; but on whomever it falls, it will grind him to powder' (Matthew 21:42,44).

Read Matthew 21:33-46

In the previous story I wrote about the birds finding safety in trees during storms. I want you to remember that I likened that tree to the Lord Jesus Christ. Just as the birds found safety in the tree, so sinners can find safety in the Lord Jesus.

Now I would like to tell you another story about a tree. Indeed it could well be the very same tree in which the birds found safety. And the situation is just the same because the story is about a thunderstorm.

Some time ago when my daughter Lisa was at work a storm appeared over the mountains. She worked in a shop and her kind husband, seeing the storm approaching, drove the car down to her place of work so she wouldn't have to walk home in the rain. Near the buildings there was a plot of land with several tall trees growing beside a fence.

Todd looked at the clouds and saw that they were not just a black colour, but noticed also a grey-green colour. Thinking there might be hail when the storm came, he decided to park the car close to the fence and under the outspread branches of the tree. I suppose he thought, 'If the birds can find safety from the storm in the tree, then the car will be protected too.'

When the storm struck it was accompanied by furious winds, heavy rain and a little hail. Several of the people who worked in the shop had also put their cars under the trees. As the storm raged they looked out of the shop windows to see if their cars were safe. Suddenly a tremendous gust of wind tore through the trees, and the very tree that was supposed to provide protection for the cars was uprooted. The car owners just watched in horror as the tree began to fall. Lisa said it all looked as if it were happening in slow motion.

Sure enough, the tree landed on her car as well as several others parked close by. A lot of damage was done to the cars and Lisa and her family had to walk everywhere for some time while repairs were being carried out.

When Lisa rang to tell us what had happened I thought of the Scripture passage that is our text for today. The very tree that provided protection for the birds was the tree that crushed the cars to pieces. It is the Lord Jesus who is the Saviour of his people. His great love is seen in his death on the cross in the place of his people. The parable you have read today speaks of the way in which people treated the landowner's son. That landowner's son represented Jesus Christ our Saviour. How he loved his people! The apostle Paul wrote of Jesus: 'I live by faith in the Son of God, who loved me and gave himself for me' (Galatians 2:20). If you can say those words then you are safe in Jesus Christ.

But our text says something quite different about Jesus. We have seen him as a loving Saviour, but he is also an angry Judge to all those who have nothing to do with him. The reading speaks of Jesus as being a 'stone'. People fall upon the stone trying to destroy it. But the stone is strong and is not broken. In fact the ones who try to break the stone hurt themselves. The stone, we are told, falls upon others and crushes them to dust. The people who are hurt by the 'stone' are the unbelievers. They want nothing to do with Jesus.

When Christ visited this earth to save sinners, wicked people put him to death. But Jesus is coming a second time and when he does return he will judge everyone. Like the birds who found safety in the tree, sinners who trust Jesus for salvation will be safe. But the very same Jesus will pour out his anger upon all who have lived for themselves.

In the parable you have read, Jesus was speaking to the chief priests and Pharisees. They should have been the very ones to welcome the Son of

God, but they put him to death. However, the warning was not just to the church leaders of Christ's time, but to all who ignore the risen Christ.

The very same tree that provided safety for the birds in a storm crushed the car in a storm. Jesus is both Saviour of his people and the one who will punish all unrepentant sinful people. Where do you stand with Jesus Christ?

Discuss

1. The reading speaks of a vineyard. What does the vineyard represent? (See Isaiah 5:7).
2. Why did Jesus Christ die on a cross *outside* the walls of Jerusalem? (See Hebrews 13:11-13).
3. Why is God an angry God towards some people? (see Psalm 11:5).

Meditate

The Mighty One, God, the LORD,
    speaks and summons the earth
    from the rising of the sun to the place where
        it sets.
From Zion, perfect in beauty,
    God shines forth.
Our God comes and will not be silent;
    a fire devours before him,
    and around him a tempest rages.
He summons the heavens above,
    and the earth, that he may judge his people
                    (Psalm 50:1-4).

Pray

1. Give thanks to God for the fact that he rules the world.
2. Give thanks to God that on the Day of Judgement all of his people will be safe.
3. Pray that your relations and friends will come to know Jesus as Lord and Saviour.

7. Making plans — an all-powerful God

'Indeed, I have spoken it; I will also bring it to pass' (Isaiah 46:11).

| **Read** James 4:13-17 |

I am sure that each one of my readers has made plans to do things that never came to pass. Our great problem is that we are not all-powerful and so we can never be certain that our plans will be realized. It is our God, Jehovah, who is all-powerful. He not only makes plans but brings them to pass.

Some years ago my brother John and I heard that the fish were biting out at sea. Fishermen were coming home with stories of great big fish being caught. The snapper were biting and flathead were to be caught everywhere. I rang John and asked him if he would like to drive to our home and spend a day on the ocean. I told him I was sure we should catch plenty of fish. John was thrilled with the idea and together we made plans for our trip out to sea.

I checked the outboard engine, caught some bait, made sure we had all our fishing gear ready and checked all our safety equipment. John was bringing plenty of food and water for the day at sea. With our plans made I went to bed knowing that John would be arriving the next day.

Well, John arrived. He was looking forward to the day's fishing. We talked all afternoon about the fish we would catch. We even drove to the beach to make sure the ocean waves were not too big to prevent us getting out. That night as we set the alarm clock for 3 a.m. we made a final check of all our gear. Everything we could do had been done. All we had to do was sleep till the alarm woke us.

It seemed no time at all before we were having breakfast and ready for the drive to the sea. The morning light was just breaking as we got into the car and set off for the beach. When we arrived it was semi-dark, but light enough to see what we were doing. Another couple of fishermen were already there, ready to launch their boat.

As we prepared the boat for launching, we watched the other boat safely make its way through the breaking waves. Then it was our turn. We stood beside the boat, outboard engine roaring, waiting for the right moment.

'Go!' we both shouted as we jumped into the boat and accelerated towards the waves. Then without warning a small wave hit the boat, turned us sideways and we gently rolled over about ten metres from the shore.

Our feet touched the bottom and we soon had the boat back on the beach. We gathered our gear together and dragged the boat back onto the trailer ready to go home. Salt water had flooded the engine. It had to be cleaned before we could use it again.

Our plans had come to nothing! When we arrived home, we had a meal in near-silence and John returned home — without any big fish and very disappointed. All the big fish were still out in the ocean, or were being caught by other fishermen.

When God made his plans he used his almighty power to ensure those plans came to pass. God told sinful Adam and Eve in the Garden of Eden that a Saviour would be sent into the world. Satan did all he could to prevent this happening. But Satan had no power to overthrow God's plans. Nor do we.

In today's reading James tells us that when we make our plans we should always say, 'If the Lord wills, we shall live and do this or that' (James 4:15).

A person once told me there is nothing we can be sure of in this life except death. But even this is not a sure thing. Maybe the Lord will return before we die and we shall go into Christ's presence without passing through death.

When we make our plans for the future we must always remember that we have no real control over what happens. God rules, and this truth we must never forget.

The God who made the world, and all things, always brings all of his plans to completion. That is why we can trust him to fulfil all of his promises and warnings.

Discuss

1. Find a prophecy God made in Old Testament times that has been fulfilled (See, for example, Psalm 22:18 and then read Matthew 27:35).
2. What does James mean when he writes, 'If the Lord wills, we shall live and do this or that'?
3. Talk about some plans you have made that didn't come to pass because you couldn't control the events.
4. Why is it that we can always rely on God's promises coming to pass?

Meditate

Your arm is endued with power;
  your hand is strong, your right hand exalted.
Righteousness and justice are the foundation of your throne;
love and faithfulness go before you
                                (Psalm 89:13-14).

Pray

1. Thank God for all his goodness to you and your family.
2. Thank God for sending Christ to be the Saviour of sinners.
3. Ask God to guide you as you go about your lives each day.

8. A few more wrinkles — an unchangeable God

'For I am the LORD, I do not change' (Malachi 3:6).

Read Psalm 102:25-28

Every morning when I get out of bed I find so many things that have changed. The grass is a little longer, the flowers have more buds on them and the leaves on the tree look a little different.

When I find my dog he is never the same. He loves playing in the wet grass and usually I find him covered in dirt. When he has his bath he is white again — for a little while. And he is growing. When I bought him he was only ten centimetres tall, but now he is fifteen centimetres high. Yes, Wags is changing!

Every morning I look in the mirror while shaving. I am never the same. I know a few more hairs are missing from my head and a few more wrinkles are appearing. I can see all of these changes if I wear spectacles, because my eyesight too has changed and without glasses I can't see very well at all.

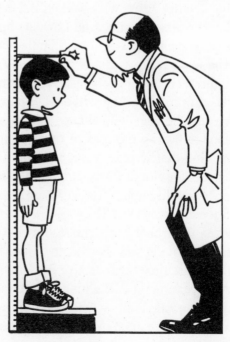

One day we met a friend we hadn't seen for many years. She looked at Valerie and said, 'You look just the same as you did when we were at high school.' But Val and I knew the truth. Yes, she had changed!

Some of the young people reading this book may think they are so young that they will never grow old. But it will happen to you too if the Lord doesn't return soon.

We have all experienced the death of loved ones. Maybe a mother or father, grandmother or grandfather, brother or sister, a husband or wife, or someone we know has died. That is the way of life. We are born into this world, grow old and die. And sin has caused this problem for us. God did not create men and women to grow old and die.

So day by day everything changes — even the strong, firm mountains change. We might think that surely the stars and planets will be there for ever. But not so. One day, when Christ returns, even this world will be destroyed and a new heavens and earth will be made.

But what about God? Well, the Bible tells us that our God never changes. His character is always the same. He has always been a God of grace, love and mercy. He has always been a just God who hates sin. God does not grow old. He is spirit and has no body that can grow old.

In Psalm 102 we read that God is always the same. This is an important truth for all of us. Because God never changes we can depend upon him. He will always carry out his promises. Again and again the Scriptures remind us that God is faithful. We make promises at times and then forget to carry them out. Not so with God. His nature never changes, so he never forgets.

And what about Jesus? Of him we read, 'Jesus Christ is the same yesterday, today, and for ever' (Hebrews 13:8). Now we are told many times in the Bible that Jesus is God. His character always remains the same. But here the writer to the Hebrews reminds his readers that the loving, caring, saving Jesus who walked the earth and was crucified is the same Jesus who was glorified and now sits upon the throne at the right hand of God in heaven. He will always be the loving, caring, saving Jesus.

The Jesus we love and worship today is the same Jesus we read of in the Scriptures. He does not change. We can depend upon him at all times because he has promised that he will always care for his people.

We are the ones who change day by day. Maybe we don't like growing old and suffering the loss of our physical and mental powers, but let us thank God that we can change. Thank God that we are not unchangeable (or, as the theologians say, immutable) as is God, because if that were the case we would remain for ever enemies of God.

But God sends his Holy Spirit into the hearts of his people and this changes their characters. Instead of hating God, they begin to love God. Instead of loving sins they begin to hate their sins. Instead of living for self and pleasure they begin to live for God and his glory.

Always remember the man called Saul — the one who would become the great apostle Paul — who said of himself: 'And I thank Christ Jesus our Lord who has enabled me, because he counted me faithful, putting me into the ministry, although I was formerly a blasphemer, a persecutor, and an insolent man...' (1 Timothy 1:12-13). Oh, reader, have you been changed by the power of God?

Discuss

1. How have you changed in the last year?
2. What is death and who dies?
3. Name the two people who entered heaven without passing through death (See Genesis 5:24; 2 Kings 2:11). Find out all you can about them.
4. What happened that changed the wicked Saul into the apostle Paul? (See Acts 9).

Meditate

Lord, you have been our dwelling-place
throughout all generations.
Before the mountains were born
or you brought forth the earth and the world,
from everlasting to everlasting you are God
(Psalm 90:1-2).

Pray

1. Thank God that he does not change and so is ever faithful to all of his promises and warnings.
2. Pray that God will never make you afraid of growing old and dying.
3. If you are a Christian thank God for changing your heart and mind.
4. If you are not a Christian pray that God's Holy Spirit will give you a saving faith in Jesus Christ.

9. A lost letter

> 'And as Moses lifted up the serpent in the wilderness, even so must the Son of Man be lifted up, that whoever believes in him should not perish but have eternal life'
> (John 3:14-15).

Read Numbers 21:4-9

Most people like a mystery.

When I was the principal of a school, I received a most important letter from the Education Department. It needed a reply within a month and required a lot of thought and planning. I read the letter in my office, told the secretary about it and asked her to keep reminding me about writing the reply.

It was the next day when she reminded me. I thought I should get on with the job. But I couldn't find the letter. We started looking everywhere for that important piece of correspondence. After searching for hours we still couldn't find it. That night at home I searched high and low, but still I had no idea where I had put it. The whereabouts of the letter was a complete mystery.

At school the following day I offered $5.00 to anyone who found it for me. And all the time I kept looking and becoming more concerned. I just had to find that letter!

The days passed. Then two weeks had gone by and still I couldn't find it. I began to think I would have to phone the Education Department and ask for a copy of that lost letter.

However, the next day, before leaving for school, I took a book from my study shelf at home. I sometimes did some reading during lunch-time. And, sure enough, there in the book was the letter! I must have had that book on my office desk and used the letter as a bookmark. The mystery of the missing letter was solved.

Now I'm sure some of you are wondering what a missing letter has to do with Moses putting a serpent on a pole. Well, read on!

The Israelites had been led out of Egypt by Moses. God had saved his people and now they were on their way to the promised land of Canaan.

Instead of being joyful about God rescuing them they began to complain. They grumbled about food and God gave them manna. And in today's reading we find the Israelites complaining about the manna they had to eat. They also complained about the shortage of water.

In the past God had provided them with everything they needed and he would do so again and again. But here we find the Israelites grumbling about God's gracious dealings with them. God's patience with his complaining people was at an end and so he sent snakes into their camping area as punishment. Many were bitten by these snakes and died.

When the people repented of their sin they begged Moses to pray to God on their behalf that the snakes would go away. God instructed Moses to make a bronze serpent and put it on a pole. Then the people were told that if they were bitten by a snake they only had to look to the serpent on the pole and they would be healed at once.

I can imagine some of the Israelites saying, 'What a silly idea! Whoever heard of a look at a bronze serpent healing snake bite?' Some, when bitten by the snakes probably said to their friends, 'Just leave me here to die. Looking at a serpent on a pole won't help me.' But then there were others who would have said to their friends, 'Moses said just a look at the serpent will save my life. Take me to a place where I can see the serpent. I must look!'

Our text for today reminds us of the death of our Lord Jesus Christ. He was lifted up on a cross and died bearing the sins of his people and suffering in their place. Jesus now invites all who realize they are sinners and want to be saved to look to him, and he will save them.

But there are people who say, 'How silly! I live a good life. I don't need to go to Jesus for salvation.' Others say, 'It's all a lot of foolishness. Just leave me here in my sins to die. Nothing can help me.' But there are also those who say, 'I'm a sinner and I need the one who is Saviour. Help me find Jesus Christ so that I might look upon him and be saved from my sins.'

To look upon Jesus means that you must trust yourself to him as the only way of salvation. You must believe in your heart that he came into the world to save sinners by living and dying for them. Jesus is a loving Saviour who invites sinners to come to him and be saved.

And what does my story about the lost letter have to do with Moses and the serpent lifted up on a pole? It is this: the whereabouts of the lost letter was a mystery to me, but I found it. Here's something for you to discover: whatever happened to the serpent that Moses made those thousands of years ago? See if you can guess. Then check your answer in the Bible.

Discuss

1. How was Jesus lifted up from the earth?
2. What is meant by the expression 'looking unto Jesus'?
3. What was the end of that bronze serpent that Moses had fixed to a pole? (You can find the answer in 2 Kings 18:4).
3. Our text speaks of 'eternal life'. What is meant by those words? (See John 10:27-28).

Meditate

The LORD works righteousness
    and justice for all the oppressed.
He made known his ways to Moses,
    his deeds to the people of Israel:
The LORD is compassionate and gracious,
    slow to anger, abounding in love

                    (Psalm 103:6-8).

Pray

1. Ask God to make you satisfied in all the joys and trials of life.
2. Thank God for giving his Son to be a Saviour of sinners.
3. Ask God to make each of you a useful member of his kingdom.
4. Pray God's blessing upon all pastors as they preach his Word.

10. What's first in your life?

'But seek first the kingdom of God and his righteousness, and all these things shall be added to you' (Matthew 6:33).

Read Luke 12:13-21

A long time ago when I was teaching in a small country school I was visited by the school inspector. I was seeking a promotion and he was visiting the school to examine my work, so that a decision could be made which would affect my future.

Towards the end of the day he sat down with me and asked me a very serious question: 'Jim, what are the priorities in your life?' I thought that he would expect me to say school life was most important, but I answered him as honestly as I could. I said, 'First comes God, second comes my church life and then comes my wife. After that my children, then my university studies and I guess school comes next.'

Some people have their priorities all wrong. Things that don't really matter seem to occupy most of their time. What are the priorities in your life? As we grow older we find that our list of priorities changes. Things that were important when we were young are not as important when we get a little older.

Christ has told us that there is one thing that should be at the top of our list and that is to find the true and living God and then through Christ gain membership of his kingdom.

Today's reading is Christ's parable about a man who had his priorities all wrong. He lived for the things of this world. The man was a successful farmer who had made a fortune. His barns were filled with the harvest and I imagine he had plenty of money just waiting to be spent.

I suppose he was a good citizen and a family man. But there was something lacking in his life. He was a stranger to God. This man had lived for his farm and the money he had piled up over the years. He had reached

39

that stage in his life when he could retire and take things easy. He thought he would now enjoy a life of ease. But God said, 'You fool! This night your soul will be required of you; then whose will those things be which you have provided?' (v. 20).

At that very moment there was only one thing that mattered to the man: 'Am I right with God? Am I ready to face his judgement seat?' Sadly, the man had made no preparation for the day of his death. All his preparations were aimed at making retirement pleasant. His priorities were all wrong.

We must always remember that there is nothing sinful in putting aside savings that will make retirement enjoyable. But at the top of our priority list must be our love of God and our saving faith in the Lord Jesus Christ. We live only a few years and this life is our preparation for eternity. Don't waste your life by living according to a list of priorities that is back to front. Your love of God must be number one. Then you can put other things in the order which are in keeping with what God expects of his people — also taking into consideration what you enjoy.

When death comes, you and I will leave behind all the things we treasure. Someone else will get those valuable objects and they might not think as much of them as we do. What we considered valuable could end up being thrown away.

40

So let us all seek God and serve him. Let us all store up spiritual treasure in God's heavenly bank. Then we shall be able to face death and judgement with a true confidence, because Jesus Christ the Judge is our Saviour. All will be well if we live by faith in Christ.

Discuss

1. Make a priority list of the five most important things in your life.
2. Now compare your lists and discuss the similarities and differences.
3. What was number 1 on the rich young ruler's priority list? (See Matthew 19:21-22).

Meditate

Man is a mere phantom as he goes to and fro:
    He bustles about, but only in vain;
    he heaps up wealth, not knowing who will get it.
But now, Lord, what do I look for?
    My hope is in you

                              (Psalm 39:6-7).

Pray

1. Thank God for all his good gifts to you and your family.
2. Pray that God might guide your parents as they watch over you.
3. Pray that you might always put God first in your life.
4. Repeat the Lord's Prayer together. Now learn it by heart.

11. Whom can you believe?

' God who at various times and in different ways spoke in time past to the fathers by the prophets, has in these last days spoken to us by his Son...'
(Hebrews 1:1-2).

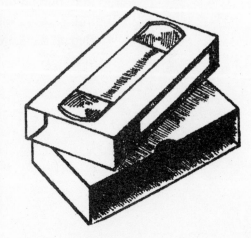

| **Read** Jeremiah 14:13-16 |

A great problem in the world today is that so many people tell lies. Lying is just part of their personality. Most people say that 'white' lies don't matter because they are just little lies and don't really hurt anyone. Some tell lies so other people are not hurt. But lies are lies. Some lies are worse than others, but all lies are sinful because God has said that we must always be truthful. We read in Proverbs 12:22, 'Lying lips are an abomination to the LORD, but those who deal truthfully are his delight.'

Some time ago in one of the Australian states a Royal Commission was held into the activities of the police force. When one senior policeman appeared before the Commissioner he was asked if he was an honourable man. He replied that he was a good policeman who always did the right thing. He was asked many times if he was telling the truth and always said, 'Yes'. In fact he seemed very upset when it was suggested that he was lying.

He was asked if he had anything to do with the buying and selling of drugs. To this he replied, 'No'. Then the head of the investigation played, for all to see, a videotape of the man buying drugs. The tape was replayed on the late evening news and it was very clear to everyone that the man was a liar. He had no idea that a video camera was recording what he was saying and doing.

We all need to be aware that God can hear all that we say and do, and when Christ returns we shall each have to give an account of what we have said and done.

Today's Bible reading concerns the judgement of God upon Judah. The prophet Jeremiah warned the people that the nation would go into captivity. God had revealed to Jeremiah that his patience with their sinfulness had come to an end and told him what would happen to the people. Jeremiah faithfully preached God's warning to the Jewish people.

But the false prophets told lies. They claimed that God had spoken to them and shown them that Jeremiah's prophecies were false. They told the people that God would not send armies to overthrow the nation. They declared that God's prophets, who told the people about the famine that would be part of his punishment, were liars. They promised the nation of Judah peace. The reading tells us very plainly what God thought of these false prophets and how he would punish them.

There have always been problems with false prophets who claim to be speaking in the name of God. Moses was warned of such false prophets and ordered that they be punished with death (Deuteronomy 18:20). And how were the people to discover if a prophet spoke God's words? God told Moses what to do. We read, 'When a prophet speaks in the name of the LORD, if the thing does not happen or come to pass, that is the thing which the LORD has not spoken; the prophet has spoken it presumptuously; you shall not be afraid of him' (Deuteronomy 18:22).

When Jesus faced the lying Pharisees, he told them that their father was the devil. He said of Satan that there was 'no truth in him... He is a liar and the father of [lies]' (John 8:44). When we are tempted to tell a lie we should remember these words of Jesus and remember that all lies come from the temptations of Satan.

The greatest prophet of all is the Lord Jesus Christ. He was, and is, the faithful and true witness of God (Revelation 3:14). He always speaks the truth and was the final prophet of God to this world. God spoke to Moses concerning Christ: 'I will raise up for them a Prophet like you from among their brethren, and will put my words in his mouth, and he shall speak to them all that I command him' (Deuteronomy 18:18).

Our text for today tells us plainly that God spoke through the prophets until the coming of Christ. When Christ began his ministry the world entered the 'last days' and God's final message to the world came through his Son. Today we have the Bible, which is God's message to all people. Many great scholars have worked very hard to translate God's message into our language. We should always thank God for their efforts.

God's words are true. They are not lies because God cannot lie (Titus 1:2; Hebrews 6:18). All of us need to read the Bible and take notice of what is written. The Bible tells of the wonderful salvation that is to be found in Jesus Christ, who is the Prophet, Priest and King of his people.

Discuss

1. Which commandment warns us against telling lies? (See Exodus 20:16).
2. Why should you always tell the truth?
3. What is one thing that God cannot do?
4. Why is Satan called 'the father of lies'?

Meditate

Let me not be put to shame, O LORD,
for I have cried out to you;
but let the wicked be put to shame
and lie silent in the grave.
Let their lying lips be silenced,
for with pride and contempt
they speak arrogantly against the righteous

(Psalm 31:17-18).

Pray

1. Thank God that his Word is truth and always dependable.
2. Thank God that we have the Scriptures in our own language.
3. Pray that God might always give you the courage to speak the truth in all situations.
4. Thank God for providing you with your daily food and other needs.

12. Don't forget to feed Truffles

'Beware of false prophets, who come to you in sheep's clothing, but inwardly they are ravenous wolves' (Matthew 7:15).

> **Read** 2 John 7-11 and 3 John 5-8

As Christians we are to do good to all people, but we have a special responsibility to our Christian brothers and sisters. All who love Jesus will do all they can to help other people who are experiencing hard times.

Of course, there are some people who will not work and expect others to give them food and whatever else they need. So, as Christians we must be sensible with our money and time and try to make sure we help those in genuine need. Many times people called at our manse seeking help. Because it was impossible to find out if their need was real, we tried to help everyone, but several times we found out later that we had been cheated by people who were just thieves.

But what has this to do with Truffles? Well, Truffles is the cat who lives in our church manse. He is a good Presbyterian cat and is really loved by the family. Recently our pastor, Peter, exchanged pulpits with my brother John. That meant they swapped homes and Pastor Peter asked John and Elizabeth if they would look after their cat, Truffles. Truffles, they said, would usually arrive home at about 5 o'clock each afternoon looking for his food. John and Elizabeth were asked to warm the milk and meat in the microwave and make sure Truffles had plenty of cat biscuits to eat.

The day after John and Elizabeth settled into the manse I had a phone call from John asking me the colour of Truffles. I told him that Truffles was a lovable, pure white cat. Then I heard John laugh and call out to Elizabeth and say, 'It's Truffles! Let him in!'

Then he told me the story of the grey cat they had found meowing at the manse door the day before. It was a lovely cat and when they opened the front door the cat trotted in. It followed them to the kitchen and enjoyed the milk and meat. Then John and Elizabeth put it to bed outside with plenty of cat biscuits.

About 2 o'clock in the morning they were awakened by a cat scratching at the bedroom window. They shouted out at it and the poor cat jumped down and ran away. When morning arrived they heard a cat meowing at the front door and when they opened the door they found a white cat who tried to run inside the house. Elizabeth pushed the cat out with her foot and closed the door.

But then they began to wonder which cat was Truffles. So John rang me to find out what was the colour of the genuine Presbyterian cat.

In today's reading the apostle John reminds us of two important truths.

First, he tells us that there are people in the world who think they are Christians yet do not believe and teach the truth of God's Word (2 John 7-11). John calls them 'deceivers'. He tells us to have nothing to do with such people. We are told that we should not even let them into our houses because they are enemies of Christ.

Secondly, John tells us that we are to welcome those who are really followers of Christ and teach the truth. 3 John is written to a man called Gaius and he is praised for helping travelling evangelists. I imagine Gaius had such people as visitors in his home. He would have given them food to eat and a bed in which to sleep. He may also have gathered people in his home so the evangelist could preach Christ to them.

So the apostle John is telling us all to give help to those who are true servants of Jesus Christ, our Saviour. We can invite them into our homes and if they need a bed for the night we should give them one. But if we have people wanting bed and breakfast while they speak lies, then we must say that they are not welcome in our homes. We need to tell them the truth of God's Word and send them on their way.

Our text reminds us that there are many 'false prophets' who sound just like true prophets. Jesus tells us that they are really wolves dressed up like sheep. They pretend to be loving people, but their teachings lead people to hell. So we all need to know what God teaches in the Bible. Then we shall be able to tell who is a true minister of Jesus and who is a 'false prophet'.

Christ's pastors show their love of Jesus Christ and by their teachings point sinners to Jesus as the only Saviour of sinners. They teach that Jesus is God — not just a god, but the Second Person of the Godhead.

That stray cat pretended to be what he was not — the Presbyterian pet cat who lived in the manse. I know that now Truffles is being well looked after. He gets into the manse whenever he wants and that grey cat is now turned away.

I pray that each one who reads these words may know the truth of God's Word and be able to distinguish Christ's 'under-shepherds' from the 'false prophets' who still get around.

Discuss

1. What does a Christian believe about Jesus Christ?
2. What is the only way of salvation? (See John 14:6; Acts 4:12).
3. Name some of the 'false prophets' we have today. How should we treat them when they come to our door pretending to be Christians yet teaching lies?

Meditate

Blessed is the man
   who makes the LORD his trust,
who does not look to the proud,
   to those who turn aside to false gods

(Psalm 40:4).

Pray

1. Thank God for leading you in the ways of truth.
2. Pray that God might open the spiritual eyes of all who believe and teach spiritual lies.
3. Praise God for sending the Holy Spirit into our hearts and minds so that we can rightly understand the Scriptures.
4. Pray for the return of the Lord Jesus Christ.

13. My thinking was wrong

'Do not forget to entertain strangers, for
by so doing some have unwittingly
entertained angels' (Hebrews 13:2).

| **Read** Genesis 18:1-8 |

In my last story you read about Truffles. When John told me the story over the telephone we both had a good laugh. When John suggested that the Truffles incident would make a good story for this book, I agreed.

Valerie then asked me what all the laughter was about. I told her the story about Truffles and suggested that the  other cat was the 'wolf in sheep's clothing'. She had a good laugh with me, but then a serious look came over her face as she said, 'Maybe that stray cat was no wolf in sheep's clothing. Maybe John and Elizabeth entertained another Presbyterian cat who was in need.'

I thought about her words and then together we spoke about the many people who had called at our manse for help. We knew we had been cheated by some of them, but we also knew that others probably were God's people who really needed help. The Day of Judgement will reveal the truth about all of those people.

As we talked, the text at the top of this page came to our minds. Then we opened the Scriptures to Genesis and read and talked about chapters 18 and 19. If you have read today's passage, you will understand that Abraham was visited by three people who he thought were men.

It was the custom of the people who lived in Abraham's day, in that part of the world, to show great hospitality to travellers. Abraham was a wonderful host to the three guests. He had water brought so the men could wash their dirty, tired and hot feet. He sat them down in the shade and had food prepared for them. When you read the story it sounds as if Abraham had his wife Sarah and his servants prepare a feast for the travellers.

In your reading you will note that Abraham had no idea that he was entertaining three from heaven — and one of the three was the LORD himself. Christ appeared in human form to speak to Abraham. Later Abraham discovered who his visitors were. If you have the time, read the whole of Genesis 18. Abraham and Sarah were promised a baby who would be an ancestor of Jesus Christ, the Saviour. God told Abraham that Sodom, because of the great sin of the city, would be destroyed by fire from heaven.

Have you ever wondered why God should have taken the trouble to come to Abraham and tell him what was going to happen to that wicked city? God didn't have to tell Abraham anything, but he did. And I believe we have the most wonderful reason given to us by Isaiah (41:8) and James (2:23). God called Abraham 'my friend'. Abraham was the friend of God! What a wonderful thing to be said about anyone — 'You are a friend of God'!

How could sinful Abraham be a 'friend of God'? The reason is simple. Abraham loved God. He trusted in God and he looked forward to the day when God's Son Jesus Christ would come to the earth to live and die so that sinners might be saved. Abraham trusted God that his sins would be forgiven for the sake of Jesus Christ.

That godly man, Abraham, showed great kindness to the strangers who came to his camp-site. He was completely unaware that he was entertaining heavenly visitors. Two of those strangers were angels and one was the Angel of the LORD — that is, Christ himself! If you read Genesis 19 you will find that Lot also entertained the two men without realizing that they were angels from heaven.

Now Christians throughout the world have opened their purses and homes to many people. They have given so much to help the needy. I don't think we have entertained angels. What happened to Abraham and Lot was something very special.

But though we have not entertained angels, we have unknowingly done things for which God will praise us one day. Jesus said, 'I was hungry and you gave me food; I was thirsty and you gave me drink; I was a stranger and you took me in...' (Matthew 25:35). And we might well ask, 'When did I ever see Jesus hungry and give him something to eat?' Jesus gives the answer to this question: 'Assuredly, I say to you, inasmuch as you did it to one of the least of these my brethren, you did it to me' (Matthew 25:40).

Truffles is now looked after very well. He is the manse cat. But when the manse is visited by that stray, it gets a little food too. Maybe it is really in need.

Never let it be said of any one of us that we failed to give help to any brother or sister in Christ. To help a Christian is like helping Christ himself. And God will reward all of his people who show kindness to others, but especially to those who are needy Christians — their brothers and sisters in Christ.

Discuss

1. Name some of the angels mentioned in the Scriptures (See, for example, Daniel 9:21; Luke 1:26; Jude 8).
2. What is the work of God's angels? (See Hebrews 1:14).
3. What happened to Lot's wife as she was escaping from Sodom? (See Genesis 19:26). Why do you think she looked back, and what has this to teach us?

Meditate

I sought the LORD, and he answered me;
    he delivered me from all my fears.
Those who look to him are radiant;
    their faces are never covered with shame.
This poor man called, and the LORD heard him;
    he saved him out of all his troubles.
The angel of the LORD encamps around those who
        fear him,
    and he delivers them

                         (Psalm 34:4-7).

Pray

1. Pray that God will give you a generous nature.
2. Thank God for his loving, generous nature in giving his Son to die for sinners.
3. Pray that the Holy Spirit will show you your sins.
4. Ask God to blot out all of your sins for Christ's sake.

14. Beware of the door!

'Then Jesus said to them again, "Most assuredly, I say to you, I am the door of the sheep"' (John 10:7).

Read John 10:7-14

Do you know how many doors there are in your house? I'm sure I could walk through our home blindfolded. I know where every door is but I didn't know how many doors we have till just now, when I counted them! In our home and garage we have fifteen doors.

Now doors are very useful. When locked they help keep out the burglars. When the door is closed we have privacy. Closed doors keep out the bad weather and in fine weather an open door allows the cool breezes to flow through the house. To get into our home we have to unlock the security door and then the deadlock on the wooden front door. Doors are the way into the rooms of the house.

Some years ago, when I was a schoolteacher, we moved to a school in the country. The day before we were to meet the parents of the children who attended the school, my wife Valerie found she had a black eye. During the night one of the children had woken up and called out for Mum. She jumped out of bed and forgetting she was in a new home walked into the half-open door. Turning on the light we found she had blood pouring out of a small cut above her eye. Very soon her eye was swollen and dark blue in colour.

We both felt very embarrassed when we met the parents of the schoolchildren. I'm sure that some thought I had punched Val in the eye. Some just laughed when I told them that she had walked into the door.

Now Jesus said, 'I am the door of the sheep.' Whatever did he mean by these words?

Jesus had been talking about sheepfolds — places where sheep could rest at night-time in complete safety. The fences were high and strong. The good shepherd would sleep across the entrance to the fold to make sure no sheep escaped into the wilderness and that no wild animals entered the fold to kill the precious sheep. The shepherd was in fact the door! Jesus was telling his hearers that he was like that sheepfold door. The only way for the sheep to enter the fold was through the door — there was no other way.

What Jesus was teaching the people was simply that if they wanted to be saved from their sins and enter the kingdom of heaven, then there was only one way — that was through faith in himself. Jesus Christ, God's Son, is the only Saviour. There is no other way into God's presence, but through Jesus.

Jesus had already spoken of some thieves and robbers who had climbed over the fence into the sheepfold. The Pharisees were teaching the people of Israel that they could only be saved by obeying God's law. We know that God's law is perfect, but no matter how well we try to obey that law we fail. The Pharisees needed to learn from Jesus the only way of salvation. They needed to go through the only 'door' in order to find salvation. Then they could teach the people about Jesus, the only Saviour of sinners.

Jesus is not only the door to the fold, but he is the one who protects the sheep. He saves his people and then takes care of them all the days of their lives. He will lead them along the pathways of holiness. Do you remember the words of Psalm 23, where David wrote of the LORD being his shepherd? He wrote, 'He leads me in the paths of righteousness for his name's sake' (v. 3).

One day, all of Christ's people will be with him in heaven. We shall be in that wonderful 'sheepfold' — the kingdom of God, prepared by Christ for his people.

In one of my other books I mentioned a book called *Many Paths — One Heaven*, in which the author claimed that it doesn't matter what religion you follow; you will one day reach heaven. This book taught lies.

Jesus said that he alone was the door — he alone was the way of salvation. Matthew records the words of Jesus: 'Enter by the narrow gate; for wide is the gate and broad is the way that leads to destruction, and there are many who go in by it. Because narrow is the gate and difficult is the way which leads to life, and there are few who find it' (Matthew 7:13-14).

Are you on the way to heaven? Remember there is only one way to heaven and that is through the narrow gate — the door — and that door is Jesus, and no one else.

Discuss

1. How many doors are there in your home?
2. Why does Jesus compare himself to a shepherd? (It may help you to understand this if you can find out something about the work of shepherds in the days of Jesus).
3. What is the only way to enter the kingdom of God?
4. On the door of which church was Jesus knocking? (Revelation 3:20).

Meditate

Know that the LORD is God.
   It is he who made us, and we are his;
   we are his people, the sheep of his pasture.
Enter his gates with thanksgiving
   and his courts with praise;
   give thanks to him and praise his name
                (Psalm 100:3-4).

Pray

1. Thank God for his care of his people.
2. Praise God that he is holy, gracious, just and a God of love.
3. If you are a Christian thank God that he saved you through Jesus.
4. Pray for the work of missionaries who take the gospel to the unsaved.

15. Up the tree in a hurry

'The name of the LORD is a strong tower; the righteous run to it and are safe' (Proverbs 18:10).

Read Psalm 144:1-8

Every person upon the face of the earth is a sinner and in danger of God's judgement. And most of these people couldn't care less. If they did, they would run to Jesus Christ for safety. Sometimes animals show more sense than humans.

If you have read my other books you will know that my brother John loves to go out in the bush with his gold detector looking for nuggets of gold. He has found many small pieces of gold, but is still looking for a really big one. Sometimes he walks about in cleared fields trying to find gold. At other times he searches in rough ground out in the bush.

One day, as John was detecting, he saw in the distance a big koala standing on the ground. The koala looked as if it was having a rest before it found a tree with juicy leaves to eat. John just looked at the big old koala who stood there half asleep.

Gradually and quietly John worked his way towards the sleepy animal and when rather close said in a very soft voice, 'Good day, old fellow.'

The koala's head suddenly lifted and its eyes searched for the source of the sound it had heard. When John spoke again the koala glared at him, but it kept very still waiting to see what he was going to do.

Slowly John stepped towards the big old koala. In a fright the animal suddenly turned, ran to the nearest tree and clawed its way up to a high branch. Then it sat down and peered at John who stood beside the trunk of the tree.

The koala was safe. It knew that John couldn't climb that tree and get to it. Up there humans, dogs and dingoes could not touch it.

In Psalm 144 David tells us that God was to him a 'strong tower'. In David's day, the kings built great walls around their cities with tall towers

within the safety of the walls. If an enemy approached, the people felt safe behind the protective city walls. And for extra safety the king could climb up the tower where he would be safe from the arrows of the enemy archers. A strong, high tower was a very important and safe place in time of danger.

The Lord was to David a strong tower of protection. When David wrote this psalm he may well have been thinking of God giving him the victory over Goliath. He could well have been remembering the many times God had protected him from King Saul and others who wanted him dead.

What amazed David was that the great God of heaven and earth was concerned about him. After all, David was just a man whose life was 'like a passing shadow' (v. 4). The same can be said for every one of us. Our lives are very short and we are sinners — rebels against God. And God is angry with all sinners.

But for sinners God has provided a place of safety from his anger. That shelter is Jesus Christ, God's only Son. It is only when a person realizes that he or she is a sinner, facing God's anger, that a place of safety is sought. And God's Holy Spirit directs that person to Jesus Christ.

Jesus, as our representative, has already paid the penalty for sin. He has been punished in the place of his people. God's great love has provided his Son to save sinners. Have you gone to God in your prayers and asked him to give you a new heart that will love and serve him? Have you confessed your sins to God and begged forgiveness for the sake of Jesus? If you have, then you are safe in Jesus Christ, who is God's protective, high tower.

May God be pleased to reveal Jesus Christ as the only Saviour of sinners to all who read these words.

Discuss

1. What is a koala?
2. Why are sinners under God's wrath?
3. Which phrase of three words is continually repeated in Genesis 5? (e.g. vv. 5,8,11,14,17). What does this teach us?
4. Why was Jesus crucified?

Meditate

For you have been my refuge,
   a strong tower against the foe.
I long to dwell in your tent for ever
   and take refuge in the shelter of your wings
                      (Psalm 61:3-4).

Pray

1. Give thanks to God that he is concerned with sinners.
2. Thank God for our salvation in Jesus Christ.
3. Pray that God's kingdom might grow larger day by day.
4. Pray for your politicians that they might rule righteously.

16. A little dog lost

'Why is it that you sought me? Did you not know I must be about my Father's business?' (Luke 2:49).

| **Read** Luke 2:41-50 |

The Feast of the Passover was a very important feast for the people of Israel. Every year at that time, the Israelites sat down to a meal of unleavened bread, roasted lamb, bitter herbs and wine to drink. This meal reminded the people of that fearful but wonderful night when the Angel of Death passed over the homes which had the blood of the lamb splashed on the doorposts and lintel. But the Angel of Death entered the homes of the rest of the people in Egypt and killed the first-born (you can read the story in Exodus 12).

The Passover feast always reminded the Jews of their great deliverance from Egypt. God had saved his people from slavery! Each year at the time of the Passover every Jew who could do so went up to the temple in Jerusalem to celebrate that great feast and so give thanks to God for his salvation.

My brother John and his family owned a little dog named Scuppers. I suppose you could call him the church dog. He played in the churchyard and each Sunday was hanging around for the worshippers to give him a pat when they left the church building. Scuppers was so well known that people who passed the manse would speak to him, and some even threw him food. He was a greatly loved dog.

But one Monday morning when Scuppers was called for his breakfast, he didn't appear. The family didn't worry too much about Scuppers' absence, but when he didn't come for lunch or for tea, everyone became concerned.

Tuesday came and still no Scuppers could be found. John and the family were starting to become very anxious about their lovely pet dog, so they drove about in the car hoping to find him. But they found no sign of Scuppers anywhere.

Wednesday came and still there was no sign of the poor little dog. Everyone was very concerned. Even some of the church members were out looking for him.

About midday on Wednesday John's wife Elizabeth went to the church building to do the weekly cleaning. When she opened the door, there was Scuppers! He jumped up at her as he was so excited to know that he had been found. I'm sure he must have been very thirsty and hungry.

Scuppers had evidently sneaked into the church building during the Sunday night service, gone to sleep somewhere and when he woke found himself trapped in the locked building.

This story reminded me of the time Mary and Joseph couldn't find Jesus who was then twelve years old. The family had visited Jerusalem for the Passover festival. A lot of people must have been travelling together because they didn't notice that Jesus was not with them on the return trip.

For three days Mary and Joseph searched for Jesus. They must have been terribly worried as they asked friends, relatives and strangers if they knew where he was. So they returned to Jerusalem and found him in the temple with the great religious scholars. He had been asking them questions as well as discussing very important biblical truths. We are told by Luke that the teachers and others with them were amazed at the knowledge Jesus had of God's Word.

Of course, Mary and Joseph were upset when they couldn't find Jesus, but they were overjoyed to find him safe and well. When Mary saw Jesus she said to him, 'Son, why have you done this to us? Look, your father and I have sought you anxiously.'

But Jesus gave his mother the reply we have for our text: 'Did you not know that I must be about my Father's business?' Jesus had come into the world to save sinners as well as to teach people about God, his heavenly Father. At the age of twelve years he was already doing his Father's work.

Now what about you and me? If you are a Christian you also will be doing your heavenly Father's business. You will be loving God with all your heart and soul as well as loving all those people about you. You will be helping those who are in need. You will be worshipping God and learning more about God each day. You will always show your love of Jesus by obeying his commandments. And when you live a godly life your heavenly Father is glorified.

Discuss

1. What did the Feast of Passover celebrate?
2. Why was the feast called the 'Passover'? (See Exodus 12:11-13).
3. Name three other festivals that the Jewish people celebrated in the days of the Old Testament. Find out something about those festivals (See Leviticus 23; Deuteronomy 16).

Meditate

I rejoiced with those who said to me,
    'Let us go to the house of the LORD.'
Our feet are standing
    in your gates, O Jerusalem.
Jerusalem is built like a city
    that is closely compacted together.
That is where the tribes go up,
    the tribes of the LORD,
to praise the name of the LORD
    according to the statute given to Israel
                    (Psalm 122:1-4).

Pray

1. Ask God to give you the grace to obey his commands and live a life that pleases him.
2. Thank God for the resurrection of Christ and for giving us a special day to worship him.
3. Pray that God might bring peace to those countries at war.

17. A safe return

'I will never leave you nor forsake you' (Hebrews 13:5).

Read Luke 15:1-10

Today's text is one of the most wonderful promises found in the Bible. God has promised all of his people that he will always be with them, no matter what the circumstances. There may be some times in our lives when we think God no longer cares about us, that he has forsaken us, but this is never the case. It is our sinful minds making us believe a lie.

Our God is the God of the living and the dead. He is always with his beloved people. God is not like any human, because there are times when people — even our friends — let us down.

You have read about Scuppers, so I would like to tell you another story about that little dog.

One day my brother John and his family had a day out in the bush. John had his gold detector with him and while he searched for that precious yellow metal, his family had a pleasant day exploring among the trees. Scuppers had a very good day chasing rabbits and digging holes.

When the time arrived for the family to leave for home, no one could find Scuppers. They called his name for a long time, but Scuppers just didn't come to the car. At long last John said, 'Well, we'll have to leave for home. I don't know where Scuppers is.'

Of course the family was very upset. So they left some bread and milk at the picnic spot in case Scuppers returned. The children gathered some grass and made a bed for their pet beside a big log. They put branches over the bed to keep any wind or rain off Scuppers if he returned.

Then, sadly, they all climbed into the car and set off for home. They loved Scuppers because he was an important part of their family. At tea time all the talk was about Scuppers and it was a very sad family that went to bed that night.

Very early in the morning, before the sun had risen the family was awake. As they sat together round the kitchen table an important decision was made — they would return to the place where they last saw Scuppers and try to find him. This decision showed how much they loved that lost dog. It meant driving over 100 kilometres (more than sixty miles) to the picnic spot.

When they arrived everyone jumped out of the car and called Scuppers' name. Big smiles soon covered all their faces when they saw a frightened little dog creep out from the branches that covered his grassy bed.

Andrew and Jenny picked up their pet and hugged him. Then the family got back into the car and began the long trip back home. Scuppers just lay on the car seat between the children and every now and again whimpered. The family thought he was saying, 'Thank you for coming back and finding me.'

Now our reading is about a sheep who became separated from the flock and got lost. The sheep had wandered off and was in real danger of being killed by wild animals. But the shepherd put the rest of the flock in a safe place and went looking for the one lost sheep. When he found it, he picked it up and carried it back to the rest of the flock. Jesus is that kind, loving shepherd who will save his people. He gave his life on the cross that sinners might be saved.

All of Christ's people need to keep close to Jesus and then they will not be lost. They need to worship with God's people. They must read the Scriptures and pray. They need to read books which teach biblical truth. When Christians wander away from other Christians they so often find themselves lost.

But the great truth is that Jesus will search out his lost people and bring them safely to heaven. He will never leave his people and will never forget them. Our God has made that wonderful promise: 'I will never leave you nor forsake you.' And our God never fails to keep his promises.

Are you safe with Jesus as your Saviour? I pray that you will be!

Discuss

1. Why do you think the angels in heaven rejoice when a sinner is saved?
2. Why would a woman be upset over the loss of one silver coin when she still had nine left?
3. Jesus was accused of eating with sinners. Why did Jesus eat with sinners? (Matthew 9:10-13).
4. Have you ever thought about having an unsaved friend over for a meal? At the table you could speak to that person about your love for the Saviour.

Meditate

I long for your salvation, O LORD,
    and your law is my delight.
Let me live that I may praise you,
    and may your laws sustain me.
I have strayed like a lost sheep.
    Seek your servant,
    for I have not forgotten your commands
                    (Psalm 119:174-176).

Pray

1. Thank God that his Son Jesus Christ died to save sinners.
2. Pray that God might bless your pastor and Sunday School teachers.
3. Pray that God might use you to gather in his straying sheep.
4. Thank God for giving us the Bible in our own language.

18. A little girl saved from death

'By this we know love, because he laid down his life for us' (1 John 3:16).

Read Luke 23:32-43

One very important aspect of the Christian character is love — love of God and love of others. And why should love be so important in the life of the Christian? The answer is very simple because the Bible tells us that 'God is love' (1 John 4:8).

One of the marks of the early Christians was the great love they had for each other. In fact we read, 'We know that we have passed from death to life, because we love the brethren. He who does not love his brother abides in death' (1 John 3:14).

In the news each day we don't hear much about love. We hear of wars, murders, riots and the many other troubles that plague our world. It is wonderful when we hear a story about someone's love for another person.

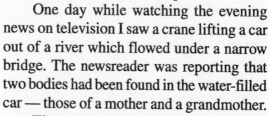

One day while watching the evening news on television I saw a crane lifting a car out of a river which flowed under a narrow bridge. The newsreader was reporting that two bodies had been found in the water-filled car — those of a mother and a grandmother.

Then two men who had seen the accident were interviewed. They had been working nearby when they saw the car skid over the side of the bridge. Both men dived into the water and swam to the car which was slowly sinking. As they tried to open the car's front doors to release the two women, the younger of the women pointed to a little girl sitting on the back seat and crying. 'Please get my daughter out of the car first!' she shouted to the men. Her mother also called out loudly, 'Save little Kim, please!'

The two men then concentrated their efforts on saving the young girl. They soon had the door opened and managed to get the small child in their arms. One of the men swam to the shore with her while the other man struggled to open the front door of the car.

But opening the back door had allowed the water to flood into the car. Soon both men were trying hard to get the front doors open, but they failed. The result was that the two women in the car drowned. They had knowingly given their lives to save their daughter and grand-daughter whom they loved dearly. The TV showed the two men weeping.

As I watched I thought of the Lord's words: 'Greater love 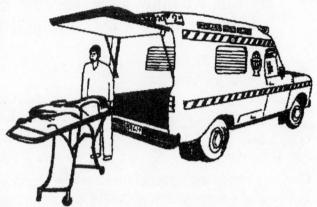 has no one than this, than to lay down one's life for his friends' (John 15:13). Those two women loved that little girl and willingly gave their lives so that she might be saved. That small child was someone very special in that family! The last scene on the TV was of an ambulance moving off with lights flashing.

I'm sure that when the little girl fully realized what had happened she would have wept for the two people who loved her so much that they had given their lives for her. Her heart would be filled to bursting with love every time she thought of them. She would never forget the love of her mother and grandmother. I'm sure you can understand this love. But the love of God for sinners is something far greater than any human love.

God loved sinners, people who hated him and wanted nothing to do with him. Paul wrote, 'God demonstrates his own love toward us, in that while we were still sinners, Christ died for us' (Romans 5:8). Sinful humans live for themselves, not for the glory of God. But God's love for sinners was so great that he determined to save a people. Christ, his Son, came into the world to die for sinners. He took the punishment due to his people. Then the Holy Spirit applied the saving work of Christ to God's people. This is love — God saving sinners, Christ dying for the ungodly! So it is that the apostle John could write, 'We love him because he first loved us' (1 John 4:19).

Today's reading is of Christ dying on a cross between two criminals. While Christ hung upon that terrible cross, bearing the sins of his people, his ears were filled with the cruel shouts of the people who cried out, 'Crucify him! Crucify him!' Satan and the demons were mocking him, thinking they had the victory in having Christ killed. In his terrible agony he saved a repentant sinner who hung upon a cross beside him. To that thief he said, 'Assuredly, I say to you, today you will be with me in paradise' (Luke 23:43).

If you are one who has faith in Jesus Christ then you know the love of God and your heart must be filled with love towards the God who saved you.

How do you know if your faith is a saving faith? There are many clues given in the Scriptures, but take notice of these words: 'If someone says, "I love God," and hates his brother, he is a liar; for he who does not love his brother whom he has seen, how can he love God whom he has not seen? And this commandment we have from him: that he who loves God must love his brother also' (1 John 4:20-21). May the love of God flood your heart.

Discuss

1. Learn John 3:16 by heart.
2. List five characteristics of a Christian.
3. How do you know if you are a Christian? (See 1 John 2:3-5).
4. Give five reasons why Christians love God.

Meditate

Because your love is better than life,
    my lips will glorify you.
I will praise you as long as I live,
    and in your name I will lift up my hands
                                    (Psalm 63:3-4).

Pray

1. Thank God for his great love as seen in Jesus Christ.
2. Ask that God will give you a real love for him.
3. Ask God to give you a love for all people — even those who hurt you.

19. A lifeline

'I am the true vine...' (John 15:1)

Read John 15:1-8

We have here another of Jesus' sayings which commences with the words, 'I am...' With this expression Jesus is claiming to be God. If you read the story of God speaking out of the burning bush to Moses you will find him asking God what his name was. The reply came back: 'I AM WHO I AM' (Exodus 3:14). The 'I AM' tells us that Jehovah is the eternal, self-existent God who rules the universe. Jesus uses the same words to show us that he is Jehovah. He is Jehovah, the Son.

In our reading and text Jesus calls himself 'the true vine'. At home we have several vines. There is the grapevine which we prune each year in order to get better fruit. We have a passion-fruit vine that has grown over the back fence and produces lovely fruit. Each year it needs pruning to encourage better growth and better fruit. But every now and again we find dead branches. We cut them off and put them on the compost heap. If the branch is not connected to the stem of the vine it dies.

Some time ago I was called to visit a man who was seriously ill in hospital. He suffered from emphysema (a disease of the lungs). He had been a smoker for the greater part of his life and the doctors told him that this bad habit was largely to blame for his illness.

Arriving at the hospital ward, I asked a nurse where I could find the man. She pointed to an oxygen cylinder with a tube attached to the top. 'Follow that tube and you'll find him,' the nurse told me. So I followed the tube and soon found myself on a nearby verandah. There the sick man sat with the tube attached to a mask over his nose.

The tube carried oxygen from the cylinder to his lungs. That tube, through which oxygen flowed, was keeping him alive. I sat down beside him and with gasping breath he told me that if the tube became disconnected from

66

the oxygen cylinder he was likely to die. As long as the oxygen flowed to his lungs he could breathe.

This is like the situation spoken of by Jesus in today's reading. If we are connected to Christ through the indwelling Holy Spirit we shall live for ever. We shall grow spiritually. Spiritual nourishment from Christ will flow into our hearts and minds.

In Christ's parable he spoke of some branches that bore no fruit. Whatever did he mean? Christ likened himself and the branches to the church. Now we all know that there are many people who attend worship who have no saving interest in Christ. They are not attached to Christ, even though they claim to be Christians. These are the branches that Jesus tells us bear no spiritual fruit. The Holy Spirit does not live in them so they are dead, useless branches. One day they will end up in God's rubbish heap — hell.

But all who are born again — united to Christ — bear spiritual fruit. These people live godly lives of obedience to their Lord and Saviour. When they fall into sin they repent and confess those sins to God and seek forgiveness. These are the people who bear witness to their love of Christ and are not ashamed to tell others what he has done for them.

And how does Jesus 'prune' his people so that they produce more fruit? I often see my wife pruning our couple of vines. If plants feel pain, then pruning must hurt. And God's pruning can hurt too.

It is not so much happiness, but holiness, that God is seeking. God may bring sadness into the lives of his people to bring them closer to himself. While I was writing this chapter, the telephone rang and I was told of the sudden death of a Christian man in our congregation. A family weeps over the death of one they loved. One son is a missionary in India and the rest of the family are spread throughout Australia. I'm sure God will use this as a pruning to bring each member of the family closer to himself. They will seek their comfort from the Lord and as he blesses and upholds them in their sorrow they will no doubt be made ready to live even more to his glory.

God's pruning can take the form of sickness, loss of friends, loss of possessions, or just difficult times when Christians cast themselves more and more upon God for help. The difficult days are the growing days for Christians. For some reason we don't seem to grow much spiritually when all is going well. Sometimes we even forget to thank God for the good times.

So the question must be asked of you: are you united to Christ through a God-given faith? Is God causing you to grow spiritually as you feast upon Christ and his Word? Are you among those whom God 'prunes' to produce more spiritual fruit?

Discuss

1 Who was Moses?
2. How can you know if you are attached to Christ as a living branch is to the vine?
3. What is the fruit of the Spirit? (See Galatians 5:22-23).
4. Why do you think we grow closer to Christ when we have difficult times?

Meditate

I lie down and sleep;
    I wake again, because the LORD sustains me.
I will not fear the tens of thousands
    drawn up against me on every side.
Arise O LORD!
    Deliver me, O my God!

(Psalm 3:5-7).

Pray

1. Thank God for spiritual blessings to family members. He promised to be God to us and our children.
2. Pray that God might bring unbelievers to a saving knowledge of Christ.
3. Confess your sins to God and seek forgiveness.
4. Pray that God will keep you faithful to Jesus.

20. Keeping promises

'When you make a vow to God, do not delay to pay it; for he has no pleasure in fools. Pay what you have vowed. It is better not to vow than to vow and not pay' (Ecclesiastes 5:4-5).

Read 1 Samuel 1:8-28

It is so easy to make promises. I'm sure every reader has at some time made a promise to someone and then failed to carry it out. Some people make promises which they have no intention of carrying out. God has something to say about making promises, or vows. Our text tells us very plainly that we must keep our vows. We are told that people who make vows and do not carry them out are 'fools'.

Today's reading is about a godly woman named Hannah. She and her husband Elkanah couldn't have a baby. Hannah was terribly upset about this so one day she made a promise — a vow — to God. She prayed that God would give her a son, 'a male child'. Then she added a promise that if he answered her prayer she would 'give him to the LORD all the days of his life...' (v. 11).

Promises are meant to be kept. In fact God says in our text that it is 'better not to vow than to vow and not pay'.

A Christian woman I know well — I'll call her Elizabeth — told me a true story about Dorothy, one of her friends. They had attended the same school and I think they must have been up to a lot of tricks when they were young. In those days they did not love the Lord, but they had mums and dads who did and who prayed every day that all of their children might become followers of the Lord Jesus. God answered the prayers of those parents and Elizabeth is now the wife of a minister.

Recently she met her old school-friend and together they laughed about the fun they had when they were young. They told one another about their lives and Elizabeth discovered that her friend was back home in Australia after spending many, many years on the mission-field as a nurse. She had also spent a lot of time witnessing to the patients and others about Jesus Christ her Saviour.

Elizabeth then asked her friend Dorothy how she became a Christian. The answer went something like this:

'When I was fifteen, I left school to get a job in a hospital. I was too young to train to be a nurse, but eventually I was given work in the local hospital. Before I left home, Mum made me promise her that I would read one chapter of the Bible every night. Even though I didn't really want to do this, I decided to keep the promise.

'A couple of years later I began training as a nurse and lived at the hospital with the other girls who were nursing. They used to laugh at me when I took out my Bible to read the next chapter. But I didn't care what they thought about me reading a chapter of God's Word each night before bed. I just wanted to keep the promise I made to Mum.

'About three years after leaving home, I was reading Psalm 51 and came to the words, "Against you, you only, have I sinned..." Suddenly I realized that all the wicked things I had done were sins against God. Then I began to cry and asked God to forgive me. God had changed my heart. I was born again. My heart was filled with the love of God and soon everyone in the hospital knew I had become a Christian!'

A young girl made a promise to her mother, and she kept that promise. God used her reading of the Scriptures to answer her parents' prayers that their daughter might become a Christian. Then God used her to do missionary work in a foreign country.

How many times has someone said to you, 'But you promised...!'? I hope you felt very guilty and then carried out your vow.

In the reading from 1 Samuel, Hannah made her promise to God. When God gave her a lovely baby boy she kept the promise she had made. I wonder if Hannah ever said to her husband Elkanah, 'Let's forget the promise I made to God and keep little Samuel here with us'? I don't believe that Hannah ever thought such a thing. In fact when Samuel was only a young boy his parents took him up to Shiloh where Eli was the priest. There Hannah said to Eli, 'For this child I prayed, and the LORD has granted me my petition which I asked of him. Therefore I also have lent him to the LORD; as long as he lives he shall be lent to the LORD' (vv. 27-28).

Promises are meant to be kept, but we so often fail to carry out what we promise to do. Sometimes we ask, 'Upon whom can we depend?' The apostle

Paul gives us the answer. He told Timothy, 'If we are faithless, he remains faithful...' (2 Timothy 2:13). God keeps all of his promises.

We are told that if we believe on the Lord Jesus Christ we shall be saved (Acts 16:31). Read John 3:16: 'For God so loved the world that he gave his only begotten Son, that whoever believes in him should not perish, but have everlasting life.'

We could go on and list hundreds of promises God has made. He will keep them all. Heaven is for all who live by faith in Jesus — hell is for all who do not trust savingly in Jesus!

Discuss

1. Earlier you were asked to learn by heart John 3:16. How good is your memory? Now repeat the words of John 3:16.
2. What promise did God make to King David that is fulfilled in Christ our King? (See 2 Samuel 7:11-16).
3. Who became Samuel's spiritual teacher?
4. Who are your spiritual teachers? Can you suggest any ways they can do more to help you?

Meditate

Sacrifice thank-offerings to God,
    fulfil your vows to the Most High,
and call upon me in the day of trouble;
    I will deliver you, and you will honour me
                            (Psalm 50:14-15).

Pray

1. Pray that your friends might come to love and serve Jesus Christ.
2. Thank God for being a God who keeps his promises.
3. Ask God to give you a real desire to read his Word.
4. Praise God for being a Saviour of sinners.

21. Ouch! That hurts!

'I gave my back to those who struck me, and my cheeks to those who plucked out the beard; I did not hide my face from shame and spitting' (Isaiah 50:6).

Read Matthew 26:67-68 and 27:27-31

Today we read something of the suffering of the Lord Jesus before he was crucified. He suffered terribly in the place of his people. He was not just being crucified — that was a horrible way to die — but he was forsaken by his Father. And we must always remember that everything Jesus suffered was in the place of his sinful people.

If you are a Christian, then Jesus suffered and died in your place. God placed your punishment upon Jesus. How you should love your Saviour!

Our text prophesied that wicked men would even pluck the hair from Jesus' beard. I'm sure that all my readers have had their hair pulled at some time and know that it can hurt very much. Even plucking out a single hair can hurt.

One morning after worship, my brother John came to the door of the church building to speak to his congregation. One lady was speaking quietly to him when she thought she could see a white thread hanging from his shirt collar. She whispered this to John and then quickly grabbed the thread and pulled. But John gave a yell: 'Ouch, that hurts!'

Why did he call out in surprise? It wasn't a white thread at all, but a white chest-hair poking over his collar.

The dear lady was horrified at what she had done and spent many minutes apologizing for her mistake. Now anyone who tries to pluck a thread from John's clothing is told to wait while he checks it out first — it might be one of his hairs and not a thread.

Why did Jesus, the only Son of God, come into this world? Paul tells us very plainly: 'Christ Jesus came into the world to save sinners...' (1 Timothy 1:15).

Sin is terrible because it is rebellion against God. We sin when we do not live as God commands. And God has told us that 'The wages of sin is death' (Romans 6:23). This is not only the death we experience when life on earth comes to an end, but eternal death, which is hell.

Jesus came into the world to live a life of perfect obedience to his Father. He did this in the place of his people. His holiness is then given to each one who puts his or her trust in him. He also died in the place of his people. He suffered our hell. Our Bible reading tells us something of that suffering. But the greatest suffering of all for Christ was when he was forsaken by his Father. For a time he could not sense the presence of God, his Father. This was hell to Jesus Christ.

If you are a Christian you will love God above all else. You will love obeying his commands which are found in the Bible. You will follow Jesus day by day. And when you sin you will repent and ask God for forgiveness.

May God be pleased to give you faith in Jesus Christ and fill your heart with love for himself.

Discuss

1. If the wages of sin is death, what is the gift of God? (Romans 6:23). Learn this text by heart, and its place in the Bible.
2. Why did the soldiers put a scarlet robe upon Jesus?
3. Why do you think the sign, 'THIS IS JESUS THE KING OF THE JEWS', was placed on the cross upon which Christ was crucified?
4. What is meant by the biblical term 'justification'? (See, for example, Romans 3:21-26; 4:1-8; Galatians 2:16). You can find the answer in my book, *A book for family reading — How to cook a crow and other stories*, or you can look it up in a catechism such as *The Shorter Catechism*, and learn the answer!

Meditate

My God, my God, why have you forsaken me?
Why are you so far from saving me,
  so far from the words of my groaning?
O my God, I cry out by day, but you do not
  answer,
  by night, and am not silent

                                    (Psalm 22:1-2).

Pray

1. Thank Jesus for coming into the world to save unworthy sinners.
2. Pray that God will forgive your sins.
3. Pray that God will give you a deep understanding of the Scriptures.
4. Ask God to help you live a godly life.

22. Homes are important

'In my Father's house are many mansions;
if it were not so, I would have told you. I go
to prepare a place for you. And if I go and
prepare a place for you, I will come again
and receive you to myself; that where I am,
there you may be also' (John 14:2-3).

Read Revelation 21:22 - 22:5

I imagine that most of my readers have a place you can call home — a place where you feel safe from the world outside. You may even have a room you can call your own. When my brother and I were young we shared our bedroom. Sometimes that caused problems, but we had a place we could call our own.

There are many people today who do not have a place to call home. I have seen people sleeping on the streets. My wife and I have had people stay overnight in our home because they had nowhere to sleep. We have all seen pictures on the TV of homeless people wandering about, especially in places where there is war or famine. If you have a comfortable home, then thank God for his kindness to you and your family.

When the Lord was young his parents had to leave their home and escape to Egypt as Herod was killing the boy babies in Bethlehem. All the male babies under two years old were killed by King Herod's men in the hope that Jesus would be amongst them. I wonder what sort of home Jesus lived in when the family were in Egypt.

We know that he had a home when his family returned to Nazareth. Joseph was a carpenter and probably built his own home. But when Jesus began his ministry we are told that he had no place to lay his head. He depended upon others to provide him with a place to sleep. Many times he and the disciples must have slept outdoors.

When I was married and our four daughters arrived we had a bigger house than we have now. The girls have left home and started their own homes with their husbands. We now have a smaller house as we don't need so much space. We have even given it a name — 'Valeni'. (Can you work out what the name means?) But even this house will be too large for us

75

when we become too old to care for the garden and keep the rooms tidy and clean. So Valerie and I sometimes talk about what we should do in the future concerning a smaller, more suitable home where we can be looked after if that is needed.

After that we shall die and the question is: 'Will there be a home for us following our death?' Our text gives us the answer. Jesus told his disciples that he was returning to heaven and there he would prepare a home for

them — and not for them only, but for all who love and serve him. Some Christians may have no home to call their own on earth, but there is a special home waiting for them with Christ.

I'm sure we all sometimes wonder what heaven will be like. Well, the Bible gives us some clues about our heavenly home. But human words can never really describe what God has prepared for his people. The apostle Paul wrote about the good things that God has ready for them. He said, 'Eye has not seen, nor ear heard, nor have entered into the heart of man the things which God has prepared for those who love him' (1 Corinthians 2:9).

The most wonderful thing about the home Christ has prepared for his people is that he will be there. Today's reading tells all Christians, 'They shall see his face.' What a glorious day it will be when we meet Jesus face to face and he speaks to us!

Won't it be wonderful to be perfect in holiness? There is no sin in the homes Christ provides. There is no more weeping and no more death in the mansion that Christ has built for his people. We shall be able to talk with all the saints who live in the dwellings Christ has prepared.

The apostle John uses the most precious stones to describe the glory of Christ's dwelling-place. On earth gold is very precious. My brother John spends many hours searching for the precious metal that is hard to find. But we are told that in heaven the very streets are paved with gold.

And on that day when Christ returns, our souls will be reunited with our resurrected bodies and we shall be with him for ever.

It's great to have a nice home here on earth, but remember that for God's people — those who love Jesus — the best is yet to be. We have a mansion in heaven waiting for us. It is my prayer that every one of my readers has his or her name on the front door of one of the homes that Christ has made for his people.

Discuss

1. Who will have a home in heaven? (See 1 Thessalonians 4:16-17).
2. Why do you think King Herod wanted Jesus to be killed?
3. Why is there no night in heaven? (See Revelation 21:23-25).
4. Talk about the good things God has in store for his people.

Meditate

Surely goodness and love will follow me
　　all the days of my life,
and I will dwell in the house of the LORD
　　for ever

(Psalm 23:6).

Pray

1. Thank God for providing for your daily needs — food, clothing, homes, friends, loved ones and those who teach you about Christ.
2. Thank God for taking away the sting of death.
3. Praise God for preparing a heavenly home for all of his people.
4. Pray for the coming of the Lord Jesus Christ.

23.   Hooked!

'And he said to them, "Follow me, and
I will make you fishers of
men"'(Matthew 4:19).

| **Read** Acts 2:36-47 |

Today's text contains the words spoken by Jesus to Peter and Andrew as
they were casting their net into the Sea of Galilee. They were fishermen
who had spent many years fishing. I'm sure they must have caught fish,
otherwise they would have given up that work long before.

Jesus called these two men to be his disciples. He would put them into
his school and teach them how to 'catch' men and women and boys and
girls. They, with the other disciples, would preach the good news concerning
Christ and so the kingdom of God would grow.

Now my brother and I caught many fish. I can only remember a few
times when we came home with no fish at all. That was one reason we
enjoyed fishing — we usually had fish for tea. During my fishing trips I
never once caught another person with my fishing hook. However I know
someone who did — by accident.

When John and his wife were on their honeymoon by the seaside, they
were visited by a close friend who wanted to spend some time fishing. John
had a boat and together the two men rowed out onto the lake and began

fishing. They didn't have
fishing rods, but used lines
rolled on a cork. With a hook
on the end and a lead sinker
not far away from the hook,
they would swing the line
around and throw it far away
from the boat. Together they
caught some lovely fish.

When swinging his line,
John's friend let it go too
quickly. The result was that
John had a fishing hook
through his cheek. His friend

Ray really was a 'fisher of a man'! With the hook through John's cheek the two rowed back to the shore and then drove to a local doctor who gently cut the hook from John's face.

When Christ called Peter to follow him and become a 'fisher of men' he meant what he said. Peter and the other eleven disciples would be taught the good news of salvation. Christ would reveal his Father to them. They would then preach the gospel throughout the world.

For just over three years the disciples followed Christ. They must have listened very attentively to all he said to them. They would have watched Christ closely as he taught the people. The disciples had the best teacher of all — Jesus Christ, the Son of God. Following the death of Christ, his resurrection and ascension to heaven, the disciples then had the work of telling the world of all the good things that Christ had done for sinners. They were truly to be 'fishers of men'.

Today's reading is the report of Peter's great sermon on the Day of Pentecost. If you have the time read the whole of Acts 2. The Holy Spirit had come into the world in all his power and glory and was working in the hearts and minds of men when Peter spoke. The result of this preaching was that some 3,000 people were saved. Before this the church had only about 120 members meeting in that upper room. Of course there would have been other believers elsewhere. The kingdom of God was growing!

I'm sure that some of those 3,000 people had stood around the cross on which Jesus hung seven weeks before and shouted out, 'Crucify him!' (Mark 15:13). But God is good. He forgives the sins of his people — even the sin of being involved in the crucifixion of his Son. Jesus had in fact prayed that God might forgive those who put him to death. We read his words: 'Father, forgive them, for they do not know what they do' (Luke 23:34).

And so the gospel net was cast out by the disciples and people were brought into the church. People began to understand that they were sinners who needed a Saviour. The apostles were good 'fishers of men' and women. They did this by telling people about Jesus himself and salvation through him. Before long the good news concerning Jesus had spread throughout the known world. Christians could be found in Israel and in all places of the Roman Empire — even in Caesar's palace. As you read the book of the Acts of the Apostles you will discover how the church grew in numbers every day.

Every Christian is called to be a 'fisher' of men and women, boys and girls. We are commanded to confess Christ to those round about us. Jesus said, 'Therefore whoever confesses me before men, him I will also confess before my Father who is in heaven. But whoever denies me before men, him I will also deny before my Father who is in heaven' (Matthew 10:32-33). Always remember that fishermen catch fish. If they didn't catch fish they would get another job or take up another sport.

Christians are to win people for Christ with the gospel. It will be a wonderful day when someone comes to you and says, 'It was because of you and what you did and said to me that I became a Christian.' May God be pleased to make us all good 'fishers of men and women'.

Discuss

1. Discuss methods you might use to tell people of their need of Jesus Christ, the Saviour.
2. How can a Christian deny Christ?
3. Why was the Feast of Pentecost celebrated? (See Deuteronomy 16:9-12).
4. Who is the Holy Spirit?

Meditate

May God be gracious to us and bless us
    and make his face shine upon us,
that your ways may be known on earth,
    your salvation among all nations
                                    (Psalm 67:1-2).

Pray

1. Pray that the gospel might be taken to all the people of the world.
2. Thank God for raising up men and women to translate the Bible into the many languages of the world.
3. Ask God to make you all 'fishers of men'.

24. The big bang!

> 'But the day of the Lord will come
> as a thief in the night, in which the
> heavens will pass away with a great
> noise, and the elements will melt
> with fervent heat; both the earth
> and the works that are in it will be
> burned up' (2 Peter 3:10).

Read 1 Thessalonians 5:1-11

There are exciting times ahead for all of God's people. The Scriptures tell us plainly that one day the Lord Jesus Christ will return and gather his people to himself. This will be a glorious day for all who love the Saviour and long for his return. The saints know that this old earth is not our final home. In fact God has promised to remake the heavens and the earth. In the new heavens and earth there will be perfection, because there will be no sin whatsoever.

Our text tells us that the heavens and earth we know will be destroyed by fire and then remade by God himself. I have often wondered what it will be like when Christ returns and this world is remade. I sometimes think it will be a huge explosion, controlled by God, out of which will come the purified new creation.

I once saw a big explosion and it was most exciting for all who were watching. When I was young my dad used to enter the rowing races at the local regatta. Nobody owned racing boats like those used by athletes today. The boats were big and heavy and rowing was hard work. But the regattas were great fun, especially for the young people who lived in and around our small country town. I can still remember that we could buy ice-cream, cakes, cordial and fairy floss. Regatta days were great days for the kids from the country. And the day was always brought to a conclusion with a huge fireworks display.

The local men had built a wooden pontoon. It had a floor about ten metres by ten metres and floated on very large drums. The pontoon was securely anchored out in the middle of the river and when night fell, three

 or four men would take out many huge boxes of fireworks. They spent time putting rockets in tubes ready for launching. They had exploding bangers, pin wheels, Roman candles, huge sparklers and many other great fireworks. We used to sit with our families on the riverbank and as the fireworks lit up the sky everybody would say, 'Oh! Ah!' as they gazed upwards. And when the fireworks display ended we all returned home excited, happy and tired.

But there was one fireworks display that I will never forget. Night had fallen and in the dim moonlight we could see the men on the pontoon getting things ready. I don't think anyone ever found out what really happened, but soon after the first firing of sky rockets a box of fireworks began to explode. Huge bangers thundered, throwing sparks into the other boxes. Within a matter of seconds we saw the best fireworks display ever. Rockets were screaming in all directions, Catherine wheels were spinning up into the sky and across the water and showers of sparks flew towards the heavens.

Then in the light we saw the men dive off the pontoon and begin swimming for the shore. It wasn't long before the flooring of the pontoon caught alight and that made a great bonfire in the middle of the river. Then there was a tremendous explosion and the pontoon blew into hundreds of burning pieces. I can still remember someone saying that the men were fortunate to escape with their lives. Apparently they had a couple of sticks of dynamite which they had intended to use to end the display.

The men later built another pontoon for the regatta fireworks, but we never saw a display like the one we called 'the big bang'! For years people told stories about that night.

But even as I sit here with a smile on my face remembering that evening I cannot help thinking about the return of Christ. We know that one day Jesus will return to earth, accompanied by the holy angels. They will gather the saints together and our new home will be made — this heavens and earth being destroyed by fire.

We should be praying for the coming of this great 'day of the Lord'. And we should always be ready for this wonderful meeting with King Jesus, our Lord and Saviour. We know what will take place and we should prepare for the day.

And how can we do that? Well, Peter tells us that we each should be living godly lives. Our faith must be resting upon Jesus our Saviour. Our longing must be for the 'new heavens and a new earth in which righteousness dwells' (2 Peter 3:13). Reader, have you a place in God's new creation? You will if you love God and live by faith in God's Son, Jesus Christ.

Discuss

1. When was the last fireworks display you attended? Why was it held?
2. Why do you think this old world must be remade? (Romans 8:20-22).
3. What is meant by the 'day of the Lord'?
4. What are the holy angels?

Meditate

Therefore, you kings, be wise;
  be warned, you rulers of the earth.
Serve the LORD with fear
  and rejoice with trembling.
Kiss the Son, lest he be angry
  and you be destroyed in your way,
for his wrath can flare up in a moment.
  Blessed are all who take refuge in him
                              (Psalm 2:10-12).

Pray

1. Pray for the return of Jesus Christ.
2. Ask God to prepare you for your meeting with King Jesus.
3. Give thanks that God is a just God who saves sinners.
4. Pray that people in heathen countries might come to know Christ as Lord and Saviour.

25. An unanswered cry for help

'Even though you make many prayers, I will not hear' (Isaiah 1:15).

Read Proverbs 1:24-29

Some people have the idea that God will always have his ear open to their prayers — that no matter when they call for help, God will come to their aid. But this is not so!

The people of Israel were God's special (covenant) people. God loved his people in a very special way. He gave them the land of Canaan as their own. And he blessed them year after year. But when they became unfaithful and began to worship other gods, he closed his ears to their prayers. Instead of blessing his people he punished them for their wickedness.

In the book of Lamentations we read the words of Jeremiah the prophet, who said of God: 'You have covered yourself with a cloud, that prayer should not pass through' (Lamentations 3:44).

I'm sure there have been times when you have been in trouble with someone and when you have spoken to that person he or she has not answered. But people are always ready to listen if you are doing the right thing. It is sad when people call for help and no one answers.

Some time ago the TV news told the story of a man whose car had crashed over an embankment and ended up upside down beside a tree. The accident happened late at night and the people living nearby didn't hear a thing. When the driver regained consciousness he found he couldn't get out of his car. His legs were trapped under the dashboard. He urgently needed help so he began to call out as loud as he could. But no one heard his cries. I guess everyone was sound asleep.

It must have been a long, cold night for the man lying injured in his car. But eventually the sun came up over the hills and he noticed vehicles moving along the road. He called out, but the drivers couldn't hear a word he shouted. The noise of the passing cars drowned out his voice.

So he called out even louder. Then at last he heard someone answer his cries. A man in a nearby house had heard him. Soon an ambulance and the police were on the scene and began the work of releasing the trapped victim. He was taken to hospital and eventually recovered. But he knew what it was like to cry out for help and not be heard.

God warned his people that sin would block their prayers from reaching his ears. The Jews began to worship false gods. Then God raised up the Chaldeans to invade the nation. This would be God's punishment of his people. And God's warning was simply this: 'I ... will laugh at your calamity; I will mock when your terror comes...' These words are found in verse 26 of our reading for today and we all need to learn from them.

God doesn't always listen to the prayers of his people. If you are living a sinful life, beware! God may decide to punish you. Your cries for help may go unanswered until you have repented of your sins.

Other people believe they can reject Christ until life is drawing to a close. They think that then they can call out to God for help and he must come to them.

In your reading you find these words: 'They will seek me diligently, but they will not find me. Because they hated knowledge and did not choose the fear of the LORD...' (vv. 28-29).

So when the Holy Spirit calls you to faith in Christ don't put off a response. It could be the one and only time the Spirit speaks to you of your need of a Saviour. If you take no notice of God's call, or say to yourself that you want nothing to do with Jesus, then God might say, 'All right, if you don't want Christ as your Lord and Saviour, I won't bother you again. In future you can call as much as you like, but I won't listen!'

You can read about Pharaoh, who saw the great miracles God performed through Moses. He saw the power and glory of God, but he took little notice of what was happening. As a consequence God hardened Pharaoh's heart so that he couldn't believe (Romans 9:17-18).

It is very dangerous to play about with God's offer of salvation in Jesus Christ. Paul warned the Thessalonians in very strong words: '... God will send them strong delusion, that they should believe the lie, that they all may be condemned who did not believe the truth but had pleasure in unrighteousness' (2 Thessalonians 2:11-12).

Today is the day of grace and Jesus says to you, 'Come to me, all you who labour and are heavy laden, and I will give you rest' (Matthew 11:28). May every one who reads these words have a saving knowledge of Jesus Christ.

Discuss

1. Why do you pray to God through the Lord Jesus Christ? (1 Timothy 2:5; John 14:6).
2. The Bible warns us not to put off the day of trusting in Jesus Christ. Why?
3. List the ten plagues that came upon the land of Egypt (See Exodus chapters 7-11).
4. Why should God take the trouble to listen to your prayers?

Meditate

I love the LORD, for he heard my voice;
  he heard my cry for mercy.
Because he turned his ear to me,
  I will call on him as long as I live

(Psalm 116:1-2).

Pray

1. Thank God for being a prayer-hearing God.
2. Thank God for providing a mediator, the Lord Jesus Christ.
3. Praise God for revealing the Lord Jesus Christ to you and your family.
4. Pray that God will use you in winning people to faith in Christ.

26. Torn newspapers

'Pursue peace with all men, and holiness, without which no one will see the Lord' (Hebrews 12:14).

Read Acts 15:36-41

We live in a world with terrible troubles. True peace is not to be found in any nation. Even when countries are not fighting each other, there are terrible crimes happening within them. Every day in the news we read and hear of riots, murders, assaults, thefts, arguments and many other troubles that happen again and again.

The Bible tells us very plainly that we are to live at peace with everyone. I pray that you are making a real effort to obey God's requirement here. If not, you must make the effort to overcome the problems you have with other people.

A farmer I met had two dogs. They seemed to get on very well with each other. Together they would round up the cattle. They didn't fight over their food and they played together quite happily. But, I was told, that was not always the case.

At one time only one dog lived on that farm and he had been taught to collect the newspaper each day. Daily a delivery van would put a rolled up newspaper in a box nailed to a post. At first the farmer, Bob, would walk down to the roadside and collect the paper. The dog then happily carried the paper in his mouth. Eventually the dog watched for the delivery of the newspaper and when he saw the truck passing he would race down to the box, grab the paper between his teeth and bring it back to the house.

When the second dog arrived on the farm everything changed. The newcomer watched the old dog collect the paper and decided that he wanted to do the same. Together they raced for the newspaper and began to fight over the privilege of carrying it home. As a result the paper was torn to pieces by the roadside. Then each dog would bring back some of the torn pages. So one dog had to be tied up and they took turns at bringing the paper to Bob. Of course the dog that was tied up would bark and howl.

Eventually Bob let both dogs try again. To his amazement they raced down to the roadside and one waited while the other took the paper from the box. Then each dog gently held one end of the rolled-up paper and trotted back to the house. They had learned to work together. Instead of fighting, peace was established. And so it is with us. We must live at peace with one another.

Much is said in the Bible about peace. We need to be at peace with God. This is only possible when Christ has paid the penalty for your sins — when you trust your salvation to Jesus. And when you are at peace with God you will find your  character is changed. You will find the fruit of the Spirit filling your life. The fruit of the Spirit is 'love, joy, peace, longsuffering, kindness, goodness, faithfulness, gentleness, self-control' (Galatians 5:22-23).

If a person knows peace with God through Jesus Christ he or she becomes a true peacemaker. And Jesus says of such people: 'Blessed are the peacemakers, for they shall be called sons of God' (Matthew 5:9). Peace comes from love. Because we are commanded to love even our enemies we can work for peace with all people.

But there are times when arguments just cannot be solved. What then? Our reading tells of a dispute between Paul and Barnabas concerning a Christian called Mark. All those involved in the dispute were Christians. They didn't punch one another on the nose and leave with anger in their hearts. They made a decision that suited all concerned. You have read about this decision in today's reading. They didn't hold grudges but each went their separate ways.

Later Paul and Mark would work together to take the gospel to people who lived in spiritual darkness. Paul calls Mark a fellow labourer in the gospel (Philemon 24). Then when writing to Timothy he said, 'Get Mark and bring him with you, for he is useful to me for ministry' (2 Timothy 4:11).

When arguments break out anywhere, they must be sorted out for the peace of all concerned. And this applies even more so in the church.

Two ladies at the church in Philippi, Euodia and Syntyche, were involved in some dispute. They weren't getting on with each other so Paul wrote in his letter to the Philippians, 'I implore Euodia and I implore Syntyche to be of the same mind in the Lord' (Philippians 4:2).

The two dogs fought over the newspaper and tore the paper to pieces. The two ladies were arguing with each other and so were tearing the church at Philippi apart. Paul said that this had to come to an end. So it is with each one of us! We are to 'pursue peace' with all people.

It might be hard to make peace with someone you don't get on with, but you must try to do so. And when you do work for peace you show that you are a son or daughter of God. You will be following in the footsteps of your Lord and Saviour Jesus Christ. After all, he came into the world to establish peace between God and sinners. May we all be peacemakers and this will be a better world as a result.

Discuss

1. How was peace established between God and men and women? (See Colossians 1:19-20).
2. What are you going to do to make friends with someone you don't like?
3. When will there be a true peace between the people of this world?

Meditate

For evil men will be cut off,
    but those who hope in the LORD will inherit
        the land.
A little while, and the wicked will be no more;
    though you look for them, they will not be
        found.
But the meek will inherit the land
    and enjoy great peace

                (Psalm 37:9-11).

Pray

1. Pray for peace between the nations of the world.
2. Thank God for the peace Christ established between God and sinners.
3. Ask again that your sins might be forgiven for the sake of the Saviour.
4. Ask God to help you to live peaceably with others, even those who are not easy to get on with.

27. Put out the fire!

'Also I say to you, whoever
confesses me before men, him the
Son of Man also will confess before
the angels of God' (Luke 12:8).

| **Read** Matthew 5:11-16 |

You have read several chapters dealing with the wonder of heaven. But do you realize that before we settle into our eternal state, whether heaven or hell, we must all stand before the judgement seat of Christ while our life is reviewed? Then, in the light of our relationship with Christ, we shall either enter the glory of heaven or be cast into hell.

Our text speaks of a wonderful moment waiting for all of God's people. That moment is when our Saviour, the Lord Jesus Christ, announces to the assembled universe that you are one of his people. All humans and angels will hear the sentence passed upon each person who has ever lived. The angels, who rejoiced when Christ's people believed, will hear Christ confess that those redeemed sinners belong to him.

We have his promise that if we confess him before men and women then he will confess before the angels that we belong to him. But, sad to say, so many professing Christians fail in their duty to confess Christ to others.

All Christians must be concerned for people who are lost and on their way to hell. Today there are so many people who live for pleasure and the things of the world. They are dancing on the edge of hell, and if they do not turn to Christ for salvation, one day they will drop into that horrible pit. How concerned are you for those lost people?

Some time ago a friend who is a pastor of a congregation was preaching. Now there are many things that distract the people who make up a congregation. Police and ambulance sirens distract their attention from the words being spoken by the minister. Sometimes people passing shout out and cause people to look towards the window or door.

As my friend was preaching he heard a beeping sound coming from the pocket of one of the men sitting in the middle of the assembled people. The man didn't seem concerned when the people sitting near him looked hard trying to find out what was causing the noise. The man and his friend quickly and quietly stood up and left the building. They were not ashamed of what had happened. It was obvious to everyone that they were needed somewhere. Later they rang my pastor friend to apologize for the disruption.

'What was the problem?' my friend asked.

'We are members of the fire brigade,' the man replied. 'The beeper was our call to get to the fire station. It turned out to be a house ablaze. By the time we arrived the house was burning well, but we soon had the fire under control and some of the building was saved.'

When my friend told me of the incident we both commented that it was great to have men involved in such an important work. They were not ashamed of their beeper going off during the worship service — a house had to be saved. They counted their work to be so important. I'm sure you would agree, but I wonder if the same people, and professing Christians generally, have a similar attitude towards the spiritually lost who are about to fall into hell. They need the saving grace of God. They need someone to take the good news of Christ to them.

Just imagine how that fire brigade would have raced to the burning house. It had to be saved! Humans are more important than houses. However, so much time, energy and money is spent saving property and very little concern is felt for the unsaved people in the neighbourhood.

May each person who reads this book fully understand that Christians have a duty to take the gospel to the lost. If you are a Christian then get on with the work of confessing Christ to your unconverted friends or neighbours.

The easiest (yet for many the most difficult) way is to open your mouth and tell people the good news that Christ came into the world to save sinners. Make sure that you are living a life of obedience to the laws of God. Then people will know that you mean what you say. Also continue to pray that God might be pleased to bless the witness you bear to your Saviour.

Never be ashamed of Christ and what he has done for you. Give him the glory and always work to win people into his kingdom.

Discuss

1. Why should Christians never be ashamed of Christ? (See Matthew 10:32-33; Mark 8:38; Romans 1:16).
2. If you are a Christian, how can you bear witness to your unsaved friends?
3. Discuss what you would say in telling someone about the salvation that is to be found in Christ Jesus.

Meditate

Come, my children, listen to me;
  I will teach you the fear of the LORD.
Whoever of you loves life
  and desires to see many good days,
keep your tongue from evil
  and your lips from speaking lies.
Turn from evil and do good;
  seek peace and pursue it

(Psalm 34:11-14).

Pray

1. Thank God for those who witnessed to you of the love of God in Jesus Christ.
2. If you are a Christian, pray for courage to tell others about Christ.
3. Pray for the work of missionaries in foreign lands.
4. Ask God to bless those who rule over us in the government.

28.   Yes, I polish the brass!

'Take heed that you do not do your charitable deeds before men, to be seen by them. Otherwise you have no reward from your Father in heaven' (Matthew 6:1).

Read Matthew 6:1-4

If you have read the Bible passage for today I'm sure you understand that God does not like boastful people.

We were commanded to confess Christ before others, but now we are commanded to do some things in secret. The text speaks of 'charitable deeds'. These are the good works we do, helping others. They come from our love of God. We don't do them in our own name so that people praise us, but rather they are done in the name of our Saviour Jesus Christ. In this way all the glory and praise goes to him.

The scribes and Pharisees were proud people. They always wanted people  to see how they served God. They paraded their good works for all to see. They even prayed in public when they had the opportunity. I can imagine the ordinary people walking down the streets of Jerusalem, pointing to the proud Pharisee praying on a street corner with arms lifted up to heaven.

Jesus told the parable of the tax collector and the Pharisee who went to the temple to pray. The Pharisee made sure everyone could see and hear him praying. Can you hear the people talking to one another? 'Look at those godly Pharisees. There they are, praying to God. I'm sure they will get to heaven — they are such godly men.'

They boasted about the good works they did and I feel sure people patted them on the back and said, 'You're a good man for what you have done. You must truly love God. And God must surely love you.' Jesus said of the Pharisees that they 'love greetings in the marketplaces, the best seats in the synagogues, and the best places at feasts...' (Mark 12:38-39).

Jesus told his followers to do their good deeds without seeking publicity. They are not to boast about their works. Christians are not to seek the praise of men and women for what they do. All is to be done in Christ's name and then Christ our Saviour gets all the praise. But God sees and knows what his people do and one day he will reward them for the acts of kindness done in his name.

At a church meeting, reports were being given by some about the work of their committee. Some told of the help that was being given to missionaries and others thanked people for doing various jobs. After the meeting was closed I heard one lady saying, 'Well, I've got something to say to Mrs ...! I helped clean the church and no one mentioned my name and thanked me for what I did!' This lady had it all wrong. She wanted the praise. She should have realized that all she did was for the Lord Jesus Christ. One day he would have thanked her for her works. However, she wanted the thanks of men and women. How sad!

In our reading Jesus told his followers that if they asked for and received the praise of men and women, they could expect no praise from God.

During our holidays Valerie and I visited a huge cathedral. It was a very big building and we decided to have a look around inside. Everything was spotless. It was very pleasant to walk quietly around looking at the massive building. Then in one corner of the building, almost out of sight, we saw a lady dressed in old clothes. She was hard at work polishing some brass rails. They sparkled brilliantly, even in the semi-darkness. We spoke to the lady and found out that in her spare time each day she came to the cathedral as she had a special job to do.

'And what job is that?' Valerie asked her.

'Oh, it's not much,' she replied. Then she pointed to the brass rails and said, 'Yes, I polish the brass. It's not much, but that's what I do to keep this building clean.'

I'm sure that as Christians we say of our works: 'It's not much, but that is what I do to serve the Lord who loves me.' Yes, we do our good works because we love the Lord Jesus, who loved us and died upon the cross to save us from the penalty of sin. We don't expect any thanks for what we do, but on that day when we all stand before the judgement throne of Christ we shall hear his wonderful words: 'Well done, good and faithful servant... Enter into the joy of your lord' (Matthew 25:21). Will you hear these words? I pray that you will.

And if others know of your acts of kindness, then make sure they understand that what you did was because you love God. In this way you will bear witness to the Lord you serve. It could well be that God uses your good works to win someone to faith in Christ.

Discuss

1. Which disciple, living at Joppa, was known for her good works? (See Acts 9:26-43).
2. Why do Christians gladly serve Jesus Christ?
3. What do you think Jesus meant by those words: 'Enter into the joy of your Lord'?
4. For whom do you think your pastor works? (See, for example, Acts 27:23; 1 Corinthians 4:1-4; Titus 1:7; Hebrews 13:7).

Meditate

I will extol the LORD at all times;
　　his praise will always be on my lips.
My soul will boast in the LORD ;
　　let the afflicted hear and rejoice.
Glorify the LORD with me;
　　let us exalt his name together

(Psalm 34:1-3).

Pray

1. Ask God to show you how you can best serve him by helping others.
2. Thank God for all the acts of love he has shown in the life of your family.
3. Pray that God will use your good works to lead others to faith in Christ.
4. Pray that governments will do all that is possible to help those people and nations that are suffering.

29. These scissors won't cut!

'For as the body without the spirit is dead, so faith without works is dead also' (James 2:26).

Read James 2:14-26

There are some books of the Bible that Christians love in a special way. Many will say that the Gospel of John is the most wonderful gospel book. Then others claim that Paul's letter to the Romans is the finest book teaching Christian doctrine.

Now we know that all Scripture is inspired by God and given to us that we might know more of him and his salvation in Christ. So we must all be students of the Scriptures.

There is one short book of the New Testament we should read again and again, because in it we are taught how Christians should live. That book is the epistle of James.

Just recently I bought a pair of scissors. Valerie told me that my use of her sewing scissors to cut paper and cardboard was ruining them. She thought it was about time I either found my missing scissors, or bought another pair for use in the study. So reluctantly I went to a hardware store and purchased a shiny new pair. I bought a cheap pair as there seemed no value in wasting money on scissors that would be used to cut paper.

When I arrived home I tried them out and found they worked perfectly. The cut was straight and there were no jagged edges. I thought I had done well in my purchase. And Valerie was so pleased that now her special pair of dressmaking scissors would be safe.

But my purchase of a cheap pair of scissors proved to be a mistake. Several weeks later when I attempted to cut some thin cardboard the screw holding the blades together snapped. So I had a broken screw and two blades. It was now impossible to cut anything with this, so I again had a problem on my hands. For scissors to be of any use both blades must be able to work together. Separate the blades and they are useless for cutting paper.

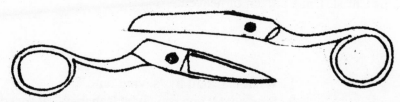

James, like the apostle Paul, taught the wonderful truth that all of God's people are saved through faith alone. There is nothing we can do to save ourselves. A God-given faith in the Lord Jesus Christ is what is needed.

However, faith that saves is never alone. Saving faith and works of righteousness go together. Jesus said, 'Not everyone who says to me, "Lord, Lord," shall enter the kingdom of heaven, but he who does the will of my Father in heaven' (Matthew 7:21). Then he told the parable of the two builders. Read this parable in Matthew 7:24-27 because it teaches us that those who hear Christ's teachings and carry them out will be saved.

Saving faith and works are like the blades of a pair of scissors. They go together. The apostle Paul put it like this: 'For by grace you have been saved through faith, and that not of yourselves; it is the gift of God, not of works, lest anyone should boast' (Ephesians 2:8-9). Here is the saving blade of the pair of scissors, but there is another blade which is called 'good works'. Paul continued by saying, 'For we are his workmanship, created in Christ Jesus for good works, which God prepared beforehand that we should walk in them' (Ephesians 2:10).

The simple truth is this: if you have a saving faith in the Lord Jesus Christ, then you will show the reality of that faith by the way you live. Saving faith is seen in the way a person lives.

So James is saying, 'If you claim to have saving faith, then your life will prove it.' You say, 'I'm saved. I have faith in Christ.' James says, 'Prove it! Prove it by your works!'

Abraham had a saving faith in God and he proved it by obeying God, even to the extent of being willing to put Isaac, his only son, to death. Rahab had faith in the God of the Israelites and she proved that her faith was real by helping the Israelite spies, who were enemies of her nation, to escape.

So is your faith in Christ a saving faith given to you by God?

Paul wrote these words to the Philippian Christians: 'Therefore, my beloved, as you have always obeyed, not as in my presence only, but now much more in my absence, work out your own salvation with fear and trembling; for it is God who works in you both to will and to do for his good pleasure' (Philippians 2:12-13).

If you are not doing the works of righteousness which come from your love of God, then your faith is a dead faith.

May we all be able to say confidently, 'Yes, I have a living, saving faith in Jesus Christ. I'm a citizen of heaven.'

Discuss

1. What is meant by 'saving faith'?
2. Find out all you can about Rahab. What part did she play in the human ancestry of Christ? (See Joshua chapters 2 and 6 and Matthew 1:5. Do you recognize any other names in the list Matthew has given in chapter 1:1-16?)
3. Why do Christians obey the commands of Christ?

Meditate

Blessed is the nation whose God is the LORD ,
　　the people he chose for his inheritance.
From heaven the LORD looks down
　　and sees all mankind;
from his dwelling-place he watches
　　all who live on earth—
he who forms the hearts of all,
　　who considers everything they do
　　　　　　　　　　　　　　(Psalm 33:12-15).

Pray

1. Praise God for his character — his holiness, wisdom, love, mercy and grace.
2. Ask God to guide you in the pathways of righteous living.
3. Ask God to give you a gentle, loving and patient nature.
4. Thank God for your family and home.

30. My outboard engine never lets me down!

'Believe on the Lord Jesus Christ, and you will be saved, you and your household' (Acts 16:31).

Read Acts 16:25-34

In everyday life we show faith in many things. When I turn on my computer I trust it to start working. I put some money in the bank and I trust the bank to keep my deposit safe for me. There were times when I was paid by cheque. Now a piece of paper with some writing on it is not much use to anyone, unless the person who signed the cheque has money in his bank account. I trusted my boss to make sure that I received money for his cheque.

There are many people whom I trust very much. I know Valerie would not let me down in any situation. I even trust Wags to behave himself when we go walking — or at least most of the time. The world can only get by on the basis of trust.

But, sad to say, there are times when people let us down. I remember once receiving a cheque which 'bounced' when I took it to the bank. The person who had written it out didn't have enough money in his account for the bank to pay me the value of the cheque.

Some time ago a friend and I went out to sea for a day's fishing. The day was not the most pleasant experience. Sometimes we would be ten miles from the coast and I wouldn't like the job of rowing home if the outboard engine couldn't be started. So before I ventured out to sea I always had the outboard tuned. It usually ran very well. I had a real faith in that outboard engine. But that particular day proved to be very frightening. We had caught

fish about five miles from the shore and when I tried to start the engine nothing happened. I checked the petrol and the tank was almost full. I put in new spark plugs and still nothing happened when I pressed the starter button.

I don't know much about engines except where the petrol goes and how to change spark plugs. So there we sat and wondered what to do. The outboard motor in which I had great faith let me down. But a trawler saw our plight and came to the rescue. I was told to check several wires and sure enough one was loose. With that back in place the engine burst into life and all was well.

There was no doubt that I had faith that the outboard would always start and get me home, but it failed me. What use was my faith in that situation? The truth is that faith is only as good as the object of faith. If we want to be saved we must have faith in that which saves.

The Pharisees trusted in their obedience to God's commands as the way of winning favour with God. But they were sinners and we know that good works — obedience — are never perfect. However, God demands perfection if we would be saved by our works. So there is no use in trusting in our good works. Going to church, praying and reading our Bibles are all good and proper things to do, but faith in them in order to win favour with God will prove a failure.

Our text tells us very plainly that we must have faith in the Lord Jesus Christ if we are to be saved. The object of our faith is the Son of God.

The question must be asked: is it possible that Christ will prove unable to save us when the judgement day comes? Is it possible that he will let his people down? The answer to this question is vital as it is not much use having faith in someone who can't really save us from our sins.

However, Jesus Christ is not just a man. He is both God and man in the one person. He is perfect. His sacrifice for sinners was perfect. Christ's sacrifice for sin was accepted by his Father. We know this because on the third day following his crucifixion Christ walked out of that tomb. The object of our faith cannot let us down, because he is God who never breaks his promises.

So Paul tells us plainly that if we have faith in Christ we shall be saved. And the apostle Peter said the same: 'Nor is there salvation in any other, for there is no other name under heaven given among men by which we must be saved' (Acts 4:12).

The *Westminster Shorter Catechism* asks the question: 'What is faith in Jesus Christ?' Then comes the answer: 'Faith in Jesus Christ is a saving grace, whereby we receive and rest upon him alone for salvation, as he is offered to us in the gospel' (Question 86).

We trust in the Christ of the Scriptures for our salvation — in nothing and no one else. Paul wrote that 'A man is not justified by the works of the law but by faith in Jesus Christ ... for by the works of the law no flesh shall be justified' (Galatians 2:16).

The Christ offered to sinners in the gospel can save and does save. And how is it that this is so? He has all power in heaven and earth and saves 'to the uttermost those who come to God through him' (Hebrews 7:25). Pray that God will give you that saving faith in Jesus Christ.

Discuss

1. What does faith in Christ mean?
2. Why was the Philippian jailer about to commit suicide?
3. Is there anyone on this earth that you can trust completely? Why?
4. Name five people who showed by their actions that their faith in God was real (See Hebrews 11).

Meditate

To you, O LORD, I lift up my soul;
    in you I trust, O my God.
Do not let me be put to shame,
    nor let my enemies triumph over me.
No one whose hope is in you
    will ever be put to shame...

                 (Psalm 25:1-3).

Pray

1. Pray that every member of your family has a saving faith in Jesus Christ.
2. Ask God to help you search your heart so that you can be sure your faith is real and centred only upon Jesus Christ.
3. Pray for the work of missionaries in foreign countries, that they might see people being saved from their sins.
4. Thank God for all the good things you have in your home.

31. Loving God

'"Teacher, which is the great commandment in the law?"Jesus said to him, "You shall love the LORD your God with all your heart, with all your soul, and with all your mind"' (Matthew 22:36-37).

Read Deuteronomy 6:1-9

One of the marks of a Christian is that he or she loves God totally. It is not just a love of the Lord Jesus Christ, but a love of God, the Three in One — Father, Son and Holy Spirit.

The Bible tells us that 'God is love' (1 John 4:8). If we are children of God, then we must be like our heavenly Father. Our lives must be filled with love for God and man. When the Holy Spirit took up residence in our souls the fruit of the Spirit began to grow within us and we should know that the first part of that fruit is love (Galatians 5:22).

Now it is difficult to love someone you cannot see, for God is spirit. Of course the Lord Jesus has a body, but he is absent from us, yet we are to love him with all our hearts, souls, minds and bodies. The same is required of our love of the Holy Spirit.

Humans do not naturally love God. They like their sins and to love God means the sinful life must be put to death. Who wants to kill something he enjoys? In order to love God sinners must be changed. And, praise God, he does change sinners. The apostle John plainly wrote, 'We love him because he first loved us' (1 John 4:19).

When I first met my future wife I was standing on a railway station waiting to catch a train to teachers' college. I saw Valerie some distance away and thought that I would like to meet that lovely-looking young lady. A friend I was with introduced us to each other and then over the months and years we found out more about each other. Val's looks and character attracted me to her.

Why do we love God?

First,we love God *out of gratitude for what he has done for us*. God chose a people to be saved. If you are a Christian I'm sure you have no idea why God chose you to be his own. It wasn't because of something that was good about you. The reason why God saved you is found in God. This thought should fill your heart with love of God.

He then sent his Son, the Lord Jesus Christ, into this world to bear the punishment for the sins of those people given to him by his Father. Christ came into the world because he loved you. He put up with the terrible abuse of men and demons. He willingly allowed wicked men to nail him to a cross where he died. As Jesus hung and bled upon the cross he did so for you. When you think about Christ's death does your heart fill with gratitude for his great love towards you as shown in his death?

Then the Holy Spirit came into your sinful body and heart and lives there. He gave you a new heart as well as the gift of faith in Christ and his work of salvation. He filled your heart with a love of God. Surely you love the Holy Spirit!

God loved sinners. If you are a Christian think about God's gracious work in your heart. You were once a sinner who wanted nothing to do with God and his Christ, but still God loved you and saved you. What a debt of gratitude you owe to God!

Secondly, we should love God *because of his character*. The *Shorter Catechism* says this in answer to the question, 'What is God?': 'God is a spirit, infinite, eternal and unchangeable, in his being, wisdom, power, holiness, justice, goodness and truth' (Question 4). We love God because he is a God of love, mercy, wisdom, kindness, truth, holiness, etc. Our new character is like that of God. Surely you love God because of his glorious character.

God is dependable and always keeps his promises. He provides for our every need.

Our God is glorious beyond anything we can imagine. I often wonder what those angels saw when they sang: 'Holy, holy, holy is the LORD of hosts; the whole earth is full of his glory!' (Isaiah 6:3).

Thirdly, we love God *because he hears and answers our prayers*.

How do you show your love for God?

First, obey the commandments of God. Jesus said, 'If you love me, keep my commandments' (John 14:15).

Second, live a life of holiness. You will hate sin and love righteousness.

Third, you will love worship. You will find true joy in praising God.

Fourth, you will serve God with your time, energy and money without complaints.

Someone gave me this poem. I don't know the author, but read it and think about it:

Only to sit and think of God—
Oh, what joy it is!
To think the thought, to breathe the name—
Earth has no higher bliss!

Father of Jesus, love's reward,
What rapture it will be,
Prostrate before thy throne to lie,
And gaze, and gaze on thee.[1]

Your life, Christian friend, must be devoted to the love of God. This is the first and the greatest commandment. May it never be said of you as it was of the church at Ephesus: 'Nevertheless I have this against you, that you have left your first love' (Revelation 2:4).

Discuss

1. Your reading mentions 'a land flowing with milk and honey'. What land was this and why is it described with those words? (See Exodus 3:8; Numbers 14:7-8).
2. What does Paul mean in Romans 12:1 where he tells us to present our bodies to God as 'a living sacrifice'?
3. How did the woman with the flask of fragrant oil show her love for Christ? (Luke 7:36-50).
4. How can you show God that you love him?

Meditate

Love the LORD, all his saints!
The LORD preserves the faithful,
but the proud he pays back in full.
Be strong and take heart,
all you who hope in the LORD
(Psalm 31:23-24).

Pray

1. Pray that God will fill your heart with love towards himself.
2. Thank God for his great love towards those he has saved from their sins.
3. Pray for each member of your family, that God will bless him or her with salvation.
4. Thank God for the Bible which tells us of our need of a Saviour and Christ's great love for sinners.

---

1. Some hymn-books include the second verse in the hymn 'My God, how wonderful thou art!' by Frederick W. Faber (1814-63) — *Publisher's note*

32. Loving others

'You shall love your neighbour as
yourself' (Matthew 22:39).

Read Luke 10:29-37

Our text is the second portion of Christ's answer to the lawyer who asked him, 'Teacher, which is the great commandment in the law?' (Matthew 22:36). Christ replied that loving others is an essential mark of a Christian.

The apostle John clearly teaches that we must love one another. He wrote, 'If someone says, "I love God," and hates his brother, he is a liar; for he who does not love his brother whom he has seen, how can he love God whom he has not seen?' (1 John 4:20).

I love my wife, but I find it hard to love the man who is a drunk and causes trouble. I find it difficult to love the girl who broke into our home and stole some of our belongings. But God tells me I must love everyone.

Our reading tells us plainly that every person is my neighbour and that I must have concern for the well-being of each. That command can be difficult to put into practice, but God has commanded that this is how his people will behave towards others.

In the parable of the Good Samaritan Jesus taught his listeners that they were to show kindness, love and mercy to all people — even their enemies. And we know that the Jews and the Samaritans didn't think much of each other. But that Samaritan showed a true love to the Jew who probably hated him.

The love I have towards my wife is one that comes from the heart and the mind. When we meet someone we love our hearts probably beat a little faster. There is a lot of emotion involved in the love between a husband and his wife. But what about the Christian who helps the drunk get home? The drunk may be saying things that are offensive. But the Christian's love says, 'This man needs help. I'll help him.'

106

Christian love isn't a love that demands that I throw my arms about a person and kiss him. Christian love demands kindness to all. It means putting up with the problems the other person creates. It means doing what is best for a person without expecting any praise or 'Thank you'. Read 1 Corinthians 13 and you will know the type of love a Christian must live out day by day in his or her relationship with others. And always remember that every act of love is done to bring glory to Jesus Christ — not to get a pat on the back from those who see what is done.

Some years ago I received a telephone call from a church elder, who was a secondary school teacher. He was very concerned about a young girl who attended the school at which he taught. She was physically handicapped and her family — Dad no longer lived with his wife and children — was in need of help. Bills had to be paid and there was a desperate need for food. But no one in our congregation had any knowledge of the family and the question was: what could we do to help those needy people?

I made a couple of phone calls to the church deacons and within a few hours one of the men was knocking on the door with a box of groceries. Also the deacons were able to pay several outstanding bills. I was able to tell the lady that we were acting out of our love for Jesus. This gave us an opportunity to talk to the whole family about the love of God for sinners. This was not the only time we were able to come to the aid of that needy family.

Later it came to my attention that one teacher at the school who had heard of the action of our church expressed his amazement that Christians would help people who had no connection with their congregation. He had ridiculed the church up till that moment, but when he saw that act of love done in Christ's name his attitude towards Christians changed.

There are many people in this sin-sick world of ours who need help and Christ expects his people to give help where they are able. It is fairly easy to show love to nice people, but Christ said that we are to love our enemies. This means we wish them well. We don't hold grudges against them and if they have difficulties, we are not to rejoice, but give them help. Now, that is hard to do. But if you are a Christian God has given you that love towards all others.

But what if someone causes you great hurt because you are a Christian? We might feel like punching him in the nose. But we will never do that if we belong to Christ. Jesus has told us that if someone slaps us on one cheek, then we turn the other to him (Matthew 5:39). And we must always be ready to forgive others for hurting us — and not just once 'but up to seventy times seven' (Matthew 18:22). This is Christian love in action.

Meditate upon the words found in Micah 6:8: 'And what does the LORD require of you but to do justly, to love mercy and to walk humbly with your God?' May Christian love fill your heart!

Discuss

1. How do family members show their love for each other?
2. Can you think of anyone to whom you could not show Christian love? Why?
3. How did Cain fail in his duty to live with other members of his family? (Read Genesis 4:1-15).
4. What is meant by the biblical word 'forgive'?

Meditate

Even in darkness light dawns for the upright,
    for the gracious and compassionate and
        righteous man.
Good will come to him who is generous and lends
        freely,
    who conducts his affairs with justice.
Surely he will never be shaken;
    a righteous man will be remembered for ever
        (Psalm 112:4-6).

Pray

1. Pray that God will give you opportunities to show Christian love towards others.
2. Thank God for the love others show towards you.
3. Pray for your minister, deacons and elders as they serve the Lord and the congregation.
4. Thank God for mums, dads and others who show so much love for their families.

33. An immovable Rock

'The LORD is my rock, my fortress and my deliverer...' (2 Samuel 22:2).

Read Matthew 16:13-20

We find rocks about us everywhere, or maybe I should say 'stones'. How often when you are mowing the lawn a stone is thrown up by the lawnmower! Those stones can travel at a great speed. I know because one cut my leg when it hit me, while another day a window was broken by a flying stone.

But there are rocks in this world that truly deserve the name 'rock'. There is the Rock of Gibraltar, that huge rock at the entrance to the Mediterranean Sea. It is a monstrous rock. Australia has a huge rock that is known throughout the world — Ayers Rock. Its aboriginal name is 'Uluru', which means 'great pebble'.

Ayers Rock is settled snugly on the ground in central Australia. It is 335 metres high, approximately 2.4 kilometres in length and 1.6 kilometres in width. If you decide to walk around 'the great pebble' you face a walk of eight kilometres. Yes, it is a big rock! Thousands of tourists visit 'the rock' each year and most of them spend hours climbing to the top.

Now Ayers Rock seems to be so huge that it could never be moved. But the fact is that it has been moved. It is lying on its side. This can easily be seen as the strata lines run up and down, not parallel to the ground. Something once flipped that rock over onto its side. I believe that the great flood of Noah's time caused the rock to fall over. Some of the sandstone from which it is formed is crumbling, too.

Many times in the Scriptures we find references to God as the 'Rock'. David called God his Rock. Now David had many enemies during his lifetime and he often had to escape to the countryside. It was when he was out on the rocky hillsides that he was able to find protection from his enemies. He hid amongst the rocks, and would have climbed huge boulders to spy out the land and discover the whereabouts of his enemies.

Some rocks were so huge they served as fortresses. There was security for those who hid in a hiding-place built upon a huge rock. Other rocks had cracks in them — maybe even small caves, and such places would be excellent as hiding-places for both animals and humans.

Because rocks were such good places for security from enemies it is easy to understand why the Bible speaks of God being a rock to his people. David said of his God and our God:

The LORD is my rock and my fortress and my deliverer...
My shield and the horn of my salvation, my stronghold.
I will call upon the LORD, who is worthy to be praised;
So shall I be saved from my enemies

(Psalm 18:2-3).

Elsewhere David said that God would put him in safety 'high upon a rock' (Psalm 27:5).

The ordinary rocks were useful to David for protection. But his greatest protector was the LORD, of whom he said, 'You are my rock and my fortress...' (Psalm 31:3).

In the New Testament we have one who also called himself a 'rock'. That person was the Lord Jesus Christ and you will have already read this in today's Scripture passage. Peter had confessed that Christ was 'the Son of the living God' (Matthew 16:16). This shows us that Peter knew exactly who Jesus was.

Christ then told Peter, and everyone who reads this passage of Scripture, that this great truth was 'the rock' on which Christ would build his church. What was the 'rock' that Christ was speaking about? It was himself! The church is not built upon our confession of faith, nor is it built upon the man Peter. It is built upon Jesus Christ, the Son of the living God. Jesus is the immovable Rock who is a hiding-place for his people.

All the rocks that we find in this world can be broken to pieces. I can only imagine what would happen if an atomic bomb was exploded just above Ayers Rock. It would probably disappear, burned to nothing in the explosion.

God is the Rock that stands firm! He cannot be destroyed! He is the perfect place of security for his people. But is it right for Christ to say that he is the rock of safety for his people? The answer is, 'Yes! A thousand times yes!'

Jesus Christ is God and man in the one person. He is the best Saviour we could ever hope for. Jesus Christ is the God who saves his people. The church is built upon him. He cannot be moved. The anger of God upon sinners will never touch us if we hide in Christ, the Rock of our salvation.

Our salvation is secure in Jesus Christ. Is your faith centred upon 'the Rock' on whom the church is built?

Discuss

1. Why does Jesus call himself 'this rock'?
2. Think of a parable which speaks about a 'rock'. What does that parable teach us? (See Matthew 7:24-29)
3. Why did David call God his 'Rock'?
4. From what can Jesus Christ save you? (See Matthew 1:21; Romans 5:9; Hebrews 2:14-15).

Meditate

The LORD is my rock, my fortress and my
    deliverer;
    my God is my rock, in whom I take refuge,
    my shield and the horn of my salvation.
He is my stronghold, my refuge and my Saviour—
    from violent men you save me.
I call to the LORD, who is worthy of praise,
    and I am saved from my enemies
                  (2 Samuel 22:1-4).

Pray

1. Thank God for the security we have in the Lord Jesus Christ.
2. Thank God for all who care for others — doctors, nurses, mums and dads and your church leaders.
3. Praise God for sending Christ into the world to save sinners.
4. Praise God for being so wonderful in his nature.

34. Beware of the bait!

'Blessed is the man who endures temptation; for when he has been proved, he will receive the crown of life which the Lord has promised to those who love him' (James 1:12).

Read James 1:12-15

From what I have written in other chapters (and any of my other books that you may have read) you will know that I enjoy fishing. During the years I have caught many fish, but of course there have been those times when I came home with nothing. Maybe the fish were not biting. It could have been that I was fishing in the wrong place. But most likely I was using the wrong bait. Certain fish like a particular type of bait, while other fish will not touch that type of food. To be a successful fisherman you need the right bait for the fish you expect to catch.

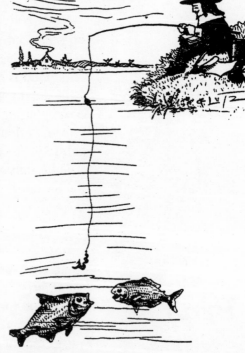

A book I was reading recently said that Satan was an excellent fisherman — he used the right bait to tempt people to sin. And so often humans take the bait that Satan has carefully chosen and prepared.

We have examples in Scripture of this fact. Think of Achan, that foolish man who was tempted by a fortune of gold and silver as well as a beautiful Babylonian coat. God had told his people they were not to take any of the treasures of Jericho for themselves. Everything was to be placed in the house of the Lord (Joshua 6:19). But Achan disobeyed God.

Think also of King David, who stole another man's wife and had her husband killed in battle. Satan used a beautiful woman to tempt David to sin.

Today's reading reminds us that God is not behind the temptations we face each day. God cannot sin. He is a holy God and sin is foreign to his character. Not only is God free from sin, James tells us that he never tempts anyone to sin.

Of course, there are people who blame God for their own sins. They argue: 'God created me with an appetite and provided tasty foods in abundance. If I become a glutton, who is to blame? It must be God for making me the way I am.'

Think of Adam after he had fallen into sin. His wife Eve gave him the fruit of the tree of 'the knowledge of good and evil'. So he ate it. He knew that God had forbidden both of them to eat that fruit, but when God spoke to Adam of his sin, Adam tried to excuse himself by saying, 'The woman whom you gave to be with me, she gave me of the tree, and I ate' (Genesis 3:12). Now we know that Eve didn't take the forbidden fruit and force Adam to eat it. Adam was unjust when he blamed God for giving him the person who handed him the fruit and told him to eat. The one to blame for Adam's eating the forbidden fruit was no one else but Adam himself.

Each one of us must bear the responsibility for our own sins. Others might be used by Satan in the temptation, but the blame for sin rests squarely upon the sinner's shoulders.

Now temptation itself is not sin. Christ was tempted, but the temptation he suffered came from outside his mind and body. Christ had a sinless nature. Satan stood before Christ and spoke to him, tempting him. Things are different with us. We have a sinful nature and we are tempted both by things outside our bodies and by the thoughts of our minds.

James speaks in our Scripture passage about our desires which 'draw us away'. Here he uses the language of the fisherman. Imagine the fish swimming along in a straight line. Suddenly it sees a juicy prawn on a hook. It looks at it and thinks to itself, 'That's just what I want.' So it turns aside, swims over to the bait, grabs it in its mouth and swallows. Before long the fish is on someone's plate being eaten. If the fish had taken no notice of the bait it would still have been alive.

Satan tempts us to love the world, not God, by making the world seem exciting and attractive. The apostle John wrote of 'the lust of the flesh, the lust of the eyes, and the pride of life' (1 John 2:16) as being the cause of so much sin. You see something you want, so you take it. Who is to blame? No one else but you! Certainly God is not to blame.

We must not be like that silly fish that took the bait and ended up on a plate, because sin that is not repented of will result in eternal death in the flames of hell.

Christian friends, we don't have to sin. We have been told that when the Holy Spirit gave us a new heart, the power of sin was broken in our lives. We became new creatures and the old way of life was gone. The apostle Paul tells us that, as Christ's people, 'We should no longer be slaves of sin' (Romans 6:6). He goes on to say that sin does not have dominion, or rule, over us (Romans 6:12,14). Christians have been set free from the rule of sin in their lives to become servants of God.

But temptation will still be there. What are we to do? Believe what God has promised: 'God is faithful, who will not allow you to be tempted beyond what you are able, but with the temptation will also make the way of escape, that you may be able to bear it' (1 Corinthians 10:13). So you see, you don't have to sin.

When temptation comes your way get your eyes off the temptation and onto the good things of God. The writer to the Hebrews gives some excellent advice concerning the Christian life: 'Let us lay aside every weight, and the sin which so easily ensnares us, and let us run with endurance the race that is set before us, looking unto Jesus, the author and finisher of our faith' (Hebrews 12:1-2).

When we sin let us go humbly to God, with repentant hearts confessing our sins and seeking forgiveness. But let us in the strength of Christ fight against sin and be victorious.

Discuss

1. Discuss some of the temptations that young people face.
2. How can they have the victory over those temptations?
3. Why did Jesus have to be tempted? (See Hebrews 2:10-18).
4. When Jesus was tempted by Satan each time he introduced his answer with the same three words. What were they and what do they tell us about where we too can find help to resist temptation? (See Matthew 4:4,7,10 and then read Psalm 119:11).

Meditate

How can a young man keep his way pure?
    By living according to your word.
I seek you with all my heart;
    do not let me stray from your commands.
I have hidden your word in my heart
    that I might not sin against you
                     (Psalm 119:9-11).

Pray

1. Pray that God might keep you from sinning.
2. Ask God to forgive each and every one of your sins.
3. Thank God for Christ's holiness given to all his people.

35. You've missed a stitch

'In the beginning God created the
heavens and the earth' (Genesis 1:1).

Read Genesis 1

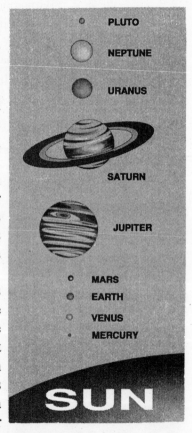

I never cease to be amazed at the universe in which I live. There is so much diversity to be found, yet everything in some way or other depends upon something else. There is colour and fragrance everywhere. Everything I touch has a different feel about it. And what about the different tastes of the food we eat? I love the many-coloured flowers with their sweet perfumes.

We look up into the sky and see the sun and moon. Then there are the planets of our solar system, millions of miles away. Things are so complex, yet everything works together so well. The size of the universe is beyond our understanding.

Our sun has a diameter of 860,000 miles and if it were hollow one million planets the size of the earth would fit inside. And the light from the sun speeds through space at 186,000 miles per second, which I have been told is six trillion (6,000,000,000,000) miles in a year. One star named Antares has a diameter of 150,000,000 miles. How can our brains comprehend such big numbers? Scientists cannot count the number of the stars. Jeremiah told us this several thousand years ago. He wrote, 'As the host of heaven cannot be numbered, nor the sand of the sea measured...' (Jeremiah 33:22). And the universe just goes on and on without any wall to mark the end of it.

This universe did not just 'happen by chance'. The Bible tells us very plainly that 'In the beginning God created the heavens and the earth.' Genesis chapter 1, which you have just read, tells you of this great creation.

We are told by the apostle John that God created everything through Christ (John 1:3). The apostle Paul wrote of Christ's works in creation: 'He is the image of the invisible God, the first-born over all creation. For by him all things were created that are in heaven and that are on earth, visible and invisible...All things were created through him and for him' (Colossians 1:15-16).

Sometimes you and I are involved in making things. I enjoy working pieces of tapestry. Recently I completed a large picture of the morning sun shining through the trees. It took quite a long time to complete and when it was finished I worked out how many stitches I had sewn. To my amazement I discovered I had done about 81,000 stitches. The work was framed and I stood back and admired my handiwork. Then someone looked closely and found a stitch I had missed. It took ages to work that one stitch into place.

But God, when he carried out the work of creation, just spoke and the world came into existence. He spoke the word and the land, seas, grasses, trees and the various animals appeared. Man was fashioned by God out of the earth.

God's creation was perfect. On the seventh day God rested from his work to contemplate all that he had done. He declared it to be 'very good' (Genesis 1:31). There was nothing missing and God did not have to repair anything in creation. Everything was perfect.

When I look at the creation round about me I am filled with wonder that my God is so powerful that he could just speak and the world burst into being. He is so wise that everything works perfectly together. His love is seen in the way he made provision for the needs of every creature.

God made Adam and Eve to communicate with himself. They were made in his image — holy and loving, with a mind able to think and make decisions, as well as to be rulers of the creation. God even came and talked with them in the Garden of Eden.

If you have doubts about the existence of God then go and have a look at yourself in a mirror and ask how life came to be. No one has an excuse for not believing in the existence of God. The proof is seen in the universe about us (Romans 1:18-23). God exists and his creation shows him to be the all-powerful, all-wise God of love.

Man ruined God's creation when sin entered the world, but there is a day coming when God will remake this world and perfection will again reign. And once again God's people will have perfect communication and fellowship with him.

When you gaze up into the heavens above and look at the world about you, what more can you say but, 'How great is my God!'?

Discuss

1. Make a list of what was created on each of the six days of creation.
2. Who was told by God that the world would be destroyed by flood? (See Genesis 6:13-21).
3. 'There is a day coming when God will remake this world and perfection will again reign.' When will that day be? (See 2 Peter 3:5-13).

Meditate

By the word of the LORD were the heavens made,
  their starry host by the breath of his mouth.
He gathers the waters of the sea into jars;
  he puts the deep into storehouses.
Let all the earth fear the LORD;
  let all the people of the world revere him.
For he spoke, and it came to be;
  he commanded, and it stood firm

(Psalm 33:6-9).

Pray

1. Thank God for the wonderful world in which we live.
2. Thank God for providing sinners with a Saviour.
3. Pray that God will give each member of your family a saving faith in Jesus Christ.
4. Thank God for his love, mercy and grace.

36. Two ears and one mouth

'Therefore, my beloved brethren, let every man be swift to hear, slow to speak, slow to wrath...' (James 1:19).

| **Read** James 3:1-12 |

James, in our text, is giving good spiritual advice to all Christians. In fact what he has to say is good advice for everyone, especially members of families and others who live together. The advice is: 'Listen carefully before you speak.'

John Blanchard quotes a saying by the rabbis of old: 'Men have two ears but one tongue, that they should hear more than they speak. The ears are always open, ever ready to receive instruction, but the tongue is surrounded with a double row of teeth to hedge it in, and keep it within proper bounds.'[1]

When James wrote these words he was speaking to Christians. He was teaching them that they were to listen carefully to God's Word and then they would be kept from saying things that hurt other people and made them angry.

I'm sure you have heard the saying: 'If someone says something hurtful to you count to ten before you reply.' Maybe it would be better if you counted to 100 before you answered.

As Christians we probably hear about 100 hours of sermons each year. That good teaching is to go in through our ears and into our hearts. Then we are to live as we are taught.

But everyone should carefully listen to this teaching by James. How many times have family members been hurt by what someone says! Cruel words, which bring tears to the eyes of others in the family, are spoken. This should not happen!

That is why James says the tongue, which causes unkind words to come out of our mouths, is like a small match which when dropped can cause a

119

devastating forest fire, resulting in tremendous damage. There is no doubt that the tongue is only a small part of the body, but it can do so much damage. The very same tongue that says, 'Thanks, Mum, for cooking tea. I love you,' can say, 'Mum, you're a nuisance. I hate you!' This is a terrible situation. James tells us the truth about our tongues when he writes that it is impossible to control that little piece of flesh in your mouth (James 3:8).

Our tongues can be used for gossip, carrying tales about other people. It doesn't matter whether they are true or false stories, we are not to pass them on to hurt those people. To do so is sin! We read in Proverbs that many people love to hear gossip: 'The words of a talebearer are like tasty trifles' (Proverbs 18:8).

Our tongues are not to be used for boasting. After all, everything we have is a gift from God. So instead of trying to praise ourselves for what we do and have, we should be thanking God. Paul asked the questions: 'For who makes you differ from another? And what do you have that you did not receive? Now if you did indeed receive it, why do you glory [that is, boast] as if you had not received it?' (1 Corinthians 4:7). So there is no point in using your tongue for boasting!

Again Paul wrote, 'Let no corrupt communication proceed out of your mouth, but what is good for necessary edification, that it may impart grace to the hearers' (Ephesians 4:29). So we are not to speak lies, or use any words that bring shame upon ourselves, other members of our family and especially upon God. We are to speak only those words which encourage people.

Now if a dog bites we can put a muzzle over its mouth. We control a horse using a bridle and bit. My boat had a rudder to control its direction. But there is very little we can do about the control of the words that fly out of our mouths — or is there? David, in Psalm 39:1, gives some good advice: 'I will guard my ways, lest I sin with my tongue; I will restrain my mouth with a muzzle...' In another place he said, 'Set a guard, 'LORD, over my mouth; keep watch over the door of my lips' (Psalm 141:3). Yes, we can control our tongues. We don't have to use them to sin.

Put two swinging doors over your mouth — one door named 'truth' and the other 'love'. Always speak the truth and make sure that all you say is the product of your love for God and man. Don't hurt people with your words. Don't sin with the words that come out of your mouth. Have the same attitude that David had concerning his speech:

Let the words of my mouth and the meditation of my heart
Be acceptable in your sight,
O LORD, my strength and my redeemer

(Psalm 19:14).

Discuss

1. Why is your tongue difficult to control?
2. What did Peter mean when he said that 'Love will cover a multitude of sins'? (1 Peter 4:8).
3. Are there some family members (or other people) that need to hear you say, 'I'm sorry for what I said'? Why not go and do it now?

Meditate

Help, LORD, for the godly are no more;
    the faithful have vanished from among men.
Everyone lies to his neighbour;
    their flattering lips speak with deception.
May the LORD cut off all flattering lips
    and every boastful tongue
that says, 'We will triumph with our tongues;
    we own our lips — who is our master?'
                                        (Psalm 12:1-4).

Pray

1. Ask the Lord to help you control your tongue and the words that come out of your mouth.
2. Pray that God will forgive any hurtful speaking you have done.
3. Thank God for your home and all who take care of you.
4. Pray that God will bless all the members of the church you attend and that they will show Christian love for each other.

1. John Blanchard, *Truth for Life,* Evangelical Press, 1986, pp.75-6.

37. I can't repair these glasses!

'Judge not, that you be not judged. For with what judgement you judge, you will be judged' (Matthew 7:1).

Read Matthew 7:1-6

Today I want you to think about what is taught in the six verses you have read because they teach important truths which in some ways appear to contradict one another. First, we are told not to judge others, and then told not to give holy things to pigs. This means you must make a judgement as to which humans are spiritual 'pigs' and who are not.

The text does not tell us we cannot judge others, but warns us to be very fair in our judgements because God will judge us using the same standard that we used to judge others. So to make right judgements we need to see clearly what we are doing.

Several days ago I met a friend who was trying to do something that was impossible and he asked me to help him out. I succeeded where he failed.

We both wear spectacles as our eyesight is not the best — we are both starting to get old! When I met him he was holding his glasses in his hand. They had fallen apart and he was trying to repair them. He was trying to balance a tiny screw on his fingernail in an effort to screw it back into a tiny hole and so reattach the lug that fitted over his ear. But he couldn't see the screw clearly, still less the hole to poke it into. So there he sat in his car trying to do the impossible. But I had my glasses on and could see what I was doing. Soon all was well. He too was wearing his spectacles and could clearly see the world about him.

Now we are commanded by Christ to take great care when we judge others. It is so easy to condemn other people.

When people are critical of others, what they are really saying is: 'I'm better than they are, as I'm not guilty of doing what they do.' Of course, they feel wonderful and very important when people gather about them to hear the latest gossip condemning others.

122

There are people who are fault-finders and enjoy telling all who will listen about other people's faults. They wrongly judge the motives of others. You know the type of people who when they see another kind person helping someone say, 'Yes, look at that person over there. He is just doing that so he can get his name and photo in the paper.' They never bother attributing the right motive to the person doing the kind deed.

Others plan to do some good work only to be discouraged by a person who condemns what they intend to do, without knowing all the facts.

If you are going to make a judgement about another person discover all the facts so you can make a righteous judgement. So often the situation is that the one who is critical of another person's small faults is a far greater sinner who refuses to acknowledge the fact. This is the person Christ speaks about who has a plank hanging out of his eye while trying to remove a tiny speck of dust out of another's eye. He simply cannot see what he is doing. He needs to clean his own eye and then he will be able to help the other person.

123

Christ was talking about the Pharisees who were always condemning others. They just couldn't see that they themselves were great sinners who needed to repent. Christ's advice to everyone is this: 'Do not judge according to appearance, but judge with righteous judgment' (John 7:24). Get all the facts before you make a judgement. And even then take great care, because you can't see into a person's heart to discover the motive for what is done.

But we must make righteous judgements every day. What are you to do when someone comes along and his teaching does not seem to agree with what you know of the Scriptures? The apostle John tells us what to do: 'Beloved, do not believe every spirit, but test the spirits, whether they are of God; because many false prophets have gone out into the world' (1 John 4:1). We make judgements based upon the facts.

And there are times when the church must make a judgement about people who are involved in a dispute. If those involved are unable to sort out their differences, the church — the elders who watch over the spiritual well-being of the members — must step in, hear the facts and make a judgement (Matthew 18:15-17).

There is a message here for each family member. Be careful how you judge one another. If a problem exists between family members, first of all get all the facts and then sort it out peacefully. That is the way to restore family harmony. May God bless your family with peace and understanding among all members.

Discuss

1. Who was Christ speaking about when he called some people 'pigs'?
2. In verse 5 Christ uses the word 'hypocrite'. What does that word mean?
3. How do you 'remove the plank from your own eye'? (v. 5).
4. The Bereans made sound judgements. Who were they and how were they able to make righteous judgements? (See Acts 17:10-12).

Meditate

God presides in the great assembly;
    he gives judgement among the 'gods':
'How long will you defend the unjust
    and show partiality to the wicked?
Defend the cause of the weak and fatherless;
    maintain the rights of the poor and oppressed.
Rescue the weak and needy;
    deliver them from the hand of the wicked'
                    (Psalm 82:1-4).

Pray

1. Pray that God will remove any critical spirit that is in your heart.
2. Ask God to fill your heart with love and kindness for others, especially the other members of your family.
3. Pray that God will give wisdom to your church leaders in all the decisions they make.
4. Pray for your pastor and his wife and children that God might bless them spiritually and make them a blessing to the church members.

38. Why did this happen to me?

'But now, do not therefore be grieved or angry with yourselves because you sold me here; for God sent me before you to preserve life' (Genesis 45:5).

| **Read** Genesis 45:1-15 |

One of the most thrilling stories recorded in the Bible is that of Joseph. His brothers hated him. He was sold into slavery in Egypt, spent time in prison forgotten by the world and yet became the most important man in Egypt next to Pharaoh. The history of Joseph is worth reading over and over again. It tells the story of God's plans being fulfilled in such a way that we can only sing the praises of the God we worship.

As far as Joseph was concerned, everything seemed to go wrong in his life. He suffered again and again, but finally he saw God's purpose in all that happened. His life was like a difficult jigsaw. The picture could not be seen clearly until the last few pieces were put into place.

Now there are many times in our lives or in our family situation when things go wrong. Maybe someone becomes seriously ill. Others lose their jobs and don't know where the money to buy food will be found. Sometimes we hear of a person being killed. The effect this has upon the family of the victim and the family of the person who was responsible for the killing is devastating. Think about the tremendous tragedy that occurs in time of war.

The fact is that there are times when the going gets tough. In those times some people cry out, 'Why me? Why doesn't God put an end to my suffering?' Others just suffer in silence and bravely put up with the difficulties knowing that there is nothing they can do to overcome the problem.

But what is to be the attitude of a Christian in times of suffering? James writes that you should 'count it all joy when you fall into various trials, knowing that the testing of your faith produces patience' (James 1:2). But none of us likes trials — they hurt — so why does God say they should be a source of joy to you? God tells us that we should not just look at our trials and difficulties and complain, but seek his wisdom so that we can see the purpose he is working through those trials.

I'm sure Joseph couldn't see any purpose in the action of his brothers when they sold him into slavery, or when Potiphar had him thrown into prison. But the day came when Joseph could say to the brothers who hated him: 'But as for you, you meant evil against me; but God meant it for good, in order to bring it about as it is this day, to save many people alive' (Genesis 50:20). In the end everything that happened to Joseph made sense. God's plans had been fulfilled perfectly.

So what about the difficulties you face in your life? Maybe you can't see any purpose in what is happening, but I assure you, Christian friend, that everything that happens in your life has a great purpose. Paul wrote these words of encouragement to suffering Christians: 'And we know that all things work together for good to those who love God, to those who are the called according to his purpose' (Romans 8:28). An important word in this passage is 'know'. It is not 'we think...' or 'suppose'! God is working out his purposes in every aspect of our lives — for his glory and our good.

Think about these words of Paul: 'We also glory in tribulations, knowing that tribulation produces perseverance; and perseverance, character; and character, hope. Now hope does not disappoint, because the love of God has been poured out in our hearts by the Holy Spirit who was given to us' (Romans 5:3-5).

What purpose, then, is to be found in the suffering of God's people?

First, *suffering brings straying Christians to their senses and they return to their God.* David wrote, 'Before I was afflicted I went astray, but now I keep your word' (Psalm 119:67). How often it is in troubled times that we walk more closely than ever with our Lord! Sad to say, it is when everything is going along smoothly that we tend to leave God to one side.

Secondly, *trials strengthen our Christian character.* This is taught in the passages of Scripture I have already quoted, Romans 5:3-5 and James 1:2. Read them again and think about their teaching.

Thirdly, *we are enabled to give help to others who suffer as we do.* We know what they are experiencing and so we can have real sympathy with them. Paul wrote that God comforts 'us in all our tribulation, that we may be able to comfort those who are in any trouble, with the comfort with which we ourselves are comforted by God' (2 Corinthians 1:4).

But always remember that in all our difficulties God is with us to provide comfort. His purposes are being perfectly worked out for his glory and the good of the saints. One day the jigsaw of life will be completed and then everything will make sense.

In your trials you should be comforted by these words from the prophet Isaiah:

When you pass through the waters, I will be with you;
And through the rivers, they shall not overflow you.
When you walk through the fire, you shall not be burned,
Nor shall the flame scorch you

(Isaiah 43:2).

Even to your old age, I am he,
And even to grey hairs I will carry you!
I have made, and I will bear;
Even I will carry, and will deliver you

(Isaiah 46:4).

Discuss

1. What are some of the trials that people suffer in life?
2. What could you do to help these people?
3. What happened to Joseph's body after he died? (See Genesis 50:22-26).
4. Read Hebrews 2:17-18 and discuss what is being taught.

Meditate

The cords of death entangled me,
  the anguish of the grave came upon me;
  I was overcome by trouble and sorrow.
Then I called on the name of the LORD:
  'O LORD, save me!'
The LORD is gracious and righteous;
  our God is full of compassion.
The LORD protects the simple-hearted;
  when I was in great need, he saved me
                                (Psalm 116:3-6).

Pray

1. Pray that God will give you support in your trials
   and tribulations.
2. Ask God to give you a heart of compassion
   towards others.
3. Thank God for all the good things he has given
   you during your lifetime.
4. Ask God to watch over all members of your
   family and keep them healthy.

39. We will serve the Lord!

'But as for me and my house,
we will serve the LORD'
(Joshua 24:15).

Read Ephesians 5:22 - 6:4

We have all lived for some time in a family. Families are not all the same, but wherever there are children there are families. The usual family is a mum and dad and one or more children. But there are many families where there is only one parent. Other children live with grandparents or other people in certain circumstances.

God's basic organization for humans is the family and God deals so often with us as families. We only have to go back to the Garden of Eden where God told Adam: 'Therefore a man shall leave his father and mother and be joined to his wife, and they shall become one flesh' (Genesis 2:24). Here was the first human family.

Then the Bible tells us of God dealing with people as family units. God saved Noah's family. When Rahab saved the spies who visited Jericho, he ensured that not only was she saved from the invading army, but her family was also saved from death.

God's dealing with Abraham is a wonderful example of his dealing with a family. God promised not only to be Abraham's God, but the God of his family as well. We read God's promise: 'And I will establish my covenant between me and you and your descendants after you ... and I will be their God' (Genesis 17:7-8). God blessed Abraham's family and his descendants after him.

The family is the basic unit of society and the congregation and you must do all you can to preserve your family.

In today's text you read Joshua's great confession. He and his family would serve the Lord. He was speaking to the Israelites after they had conquered the land of Canaan and warned them of the dangers of deserting the LORD and turning to the gods of the nations round about. Joshua knew what he was going to do. He had followed and served the LORD all his life and things were not going to change now that he had settled into his new homeland. He also knew his family and committed them to the faithful service of his God.

What a joy it is to see families coming to church! In come mum and dad, grandmother and grandfather and the children. They take their seats where they worship God, listening to the minister teaching God's truth. Together they sing the praises of their God. They take part in the activities of the congregation as a family as well as individuals.

All Christian parents have the great desire to see their children come to faith in Christ. They pray for this and they faithfully teach their children the truths of God's Word. Those mums and dads long for the day when their children will say, 'I am a Christian. I have repented of my sins and now follow Christ.'

But Christian parents are just like Joshua. As our children are growing we openly and without shame say, 'As for me and my family, we will serve the Lord.' Christian parents rejoice and give thanks to God for the salvation of their children. But they weep when any of their children turn away from the God they love and serve.

Children, pray that God will show you your sins and then look to Jesus Christ for salvation. Remember what Jesus said to Nicodemus: 'As Moses lifted up the serpent in the wilderness, even so must the Son of Man be lifted up, that whoever believes in him should not perish but have eternal life' (John 3:14-15).

Our saving God says,

And there is no other God besides me,
A just God and a Saviour;
There is none besides me.
Look to me, and be saved,
All you ends of the earth!

(Isaiah 45:21-22).

Paul's advice in today's reading must be acted upon so you can truly say, 'My family serves Jesus Christ.'

There is always hope for family members who have turned from God to the things of the world. There is a story about William Grimshaw, a godly minister who is known for announcing Psalm 119 to be sung while he rounded up people for the church service. When he died he left a godless son behind. But God answered the prayers of William Grimshaw for his son. The last words the son is supposed to have said as he was dying were: 'What will my old father say when he sees me in heaven?'

May God bless your family as you read this book. May every family member be blessed by God with a love for the Lord Jesus Christ and may the head of the family be able to stand up now in front of the family and say with Joshua of old, 'But as for me and my house, we will serve the LORD!'

Discuss

1. What was the greatest promise that God made to Abraham and his descendants? (See Genesis 17:1-14 and especially note v. 7).
2. Find out the names of any of your ancestors who were Christians. Do you think you have anything for which to thank them?
3. Find out all you can about Joshua (You will find him mentioned in, among other places, Exodus 17:8-13; 24:13; 33:11; Numbers 14:1-10, 26-38; 27:18-23; Deuteronomy 34:9 as well as the book of Joshua). Why would we call him a great man of God?

Meditate

Walk about Zion, go round her,
   count her towers,
consider well her ramparts,
   view her citadels,
   that you may tell of them to the next generation.
For this God is our God for ever and ever;
   he will be our guide even to the end
                (Psalm 48:12-14).

Pray

1. Thank God for all the blessings he has given to your family.
2. Ask God to give saving faith to each member of your family.
3. Thank God for all who take care of you in your family and the church family.
4. Pray for God's wisdom to be given to parents as they train their children in the ways of the Lord.

40. Turn on your hearing aid!

'For whom he foreknew, he also predestined to be conformed to the image of his Son... Moreover whom he predestined, these he also called; whom he called, these he also justified; and whom he justified, these he also glorified' (Romans 8:29-30).

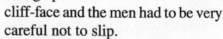
Read Matthew 13:10-16

There are a lot of people today going around with bits of plastic and batteries stuck in their earholes. It sounds silly, doesn't it? But of course we know that those people have hearing difficulties and wear hearing aids. But the hearing aid will serve no purpose if the batteries are flat.

Some time ago I read of three fishermen who were walking down a narrow track towards their favourite fishing spot. The track was down a cliff-face and the men had to be very careful not to slip.

Suddenly the man walking along behind the others saw some rocks falling. He shouted to his companions to crouch down and hang on tightly to the tree roots poking through the rocks and soil. One man did exactly as his friend told him and all was well. But the other man kept on walking and was knocked from the pathway by the falling rocks. He broke a bone in his leg and had to be winched to the top of the cliff and then transported to hospital.

His friend asked him, 'Stewart, why didn't you listen when I called out?'

Stewart's reply was, 'I heard you call, but couldn't make out your words. The batteries in my hearing aid are almost flat and I didn't have time to put in new ones.' Poor old Stewart — he could hear some sounds, but could not understand the words. I'm sure he will have fully charged batteries in his hearing aid the next time he goes fishing.

Christ spoke of people who could hear what he said, but could not understand the truth contained in his words. We read Christ's parables and say, 'I can understand what Christ is saying.' But do you really understand? Or do you just hear the words? A person who truly hears Christ's words is one who understands what is being taught and then not only loves the speaker, Jesus Christ, but obeys his teachings.

No one can understand the spiritual teaching of the Bible unless he or she is born again (we shall deal with this in more detail in the next chapter). Paul wrote, 'But the natural man does not receive the things of the Spirit of God, for they are foolishness to him; nor can he know them, because they are spiritually discerned' (1 Corinthians 2:14).

God calls men and women, boys and girls to repentance and faith in Christ, but most people take no notice of God's calling. But, praise God, some do. Our text tells us that all of those whom God loves, the ones he foreknew, are called in such a way that they believe the gospel. Like a person whose hearing aid has fully charged batteries, they can hear plainly, because God has so changed their nature that they spiritually understand what God's Word is saying to them.

Before anyone can hear God's call and respond, God must change his or her nature. Then, and only then, will spiritual truth mean anything to that person.

If you are not a Christian then pray that God might give you hearing ears so you can say, 'Yes,' to Christ's invitation to believe the good news about salvation through faith.

God calls people through the preaching of the Word on Sunday. He calls you while you read this book which speaks about your sinful nature and your need of a Saviour. He calls you when you read the Bible. But you will only say, 'Yes,' to God when the Holy Spirit changes your heart.

May you hear the call of God to come to the Lord Jesus Christ, not just with your ears, but with your ears and heart. Then you can do nothing else but run to Jesus to find salvation.

When God sets his love on anyone it means that person has been chosen to be a son or daughter of the living God. God then savingly calls him or her to faith in Christ. The destiny of these people is to be glorified in the presence of God.

It would be a real tragedy to read the Bible, go to a church where the gospel is preached and walk away not really caring about your eternal well-being. May you hear God's call to repentance and faith in Christ.

Discuss

1. Read Romans 8:29 carefully and talk about God's purpose in predestining anyone to be saved.
2. Why did Christ speak in parables?
3. The prophecy in your reading comes from Isaiah 6:9-10. What did the words mean to Isaiah?

Meditate

Let your hand rest on the man at your right hand,
 the son of man you have raised up for yourself.
Then we will not turn away from you;
 revive us, and we will call on your name.
Restore us, O LORD God Almighty;
 make your face shine upon us,
 that we may be saved

(Psalm 80:17-19).

Pray

1. If you are not yet a Christian, pray that God will so change your heart that you will be able to respond to his call to faith in Christ.
2. If you are a Christian thank God for your salvation and ask him to help you understand what he is saying to you in the Bible.
3. Thank God for your home and all who take care of you.
4. Ask God to bless the work of the missionaries who have taken the good news of Christ to foreign lands.

41. A dog wearing clothes!

'Most assuredly, I say to you, unless one is born again, he cannot see the kingdom of God' (John 3:3).

Read John 3:1-17

Nicodemus the Pharisee was one of the great spiritual teachers in Israel when Jesus walked the earth. He had probably seen Jesus and heard him speaking to the people. As the Pharisees hated Jesus and his teachings, Nicodemus must have been afraid of being seen talking to Christ. So he went to Jesus at night-time to find out all he could about this man who claimed to be the long-awaited Messiah.

Christ told Nicodemus that he needed to be 'born again' if he wanted to become a member of the kingdom of God. Poor Nicodemus didn't know what Jesus was talking about? Do you? If you want to become a member of the kingdom of God you too must be born again. You must become a new person.

As I have already mentioned, my brother John and his family had a little dog called Scuppers, who was very much loved and very spoilt by the family. Sometimes they dressed Scuppers in clothes. They put a small pair

of shorts on his back half and a very small shirt on his front half. Scuppers would run around the yard dressed as a human. He looked very funny.

Some people who had parked their car in front of the manse drove off, only to be chased by a small dog dressed in a child's clothes. John told me he heard several children in the car laughing and calling out to their mum and dad, 'Look! There's a dog chasing our car and it's wearing clothes!'

136

Poor old Scuppers! Even when dressed in the best of human clothes he was still a dog with the habits of all dogs. He still chased cats and dug holes in the garden. He still chased cars when he had the opportunity and always walked on four feet. He was a dog and no one could change his nature.

Jesus told Nicodemus that if he wanted to be saved he needed to be born again — he needed a new nature. But no one could change his spiritual nature. This was the work of God alone.

When Nicodemus was told this he couldn't believe what he heard. He should have known. After all, he was one of the great teachers of the Old Testament and there he would have read about the need sinners have of a new heart which only God could give. Ezekiel wrote God's words: 'I will give you a new heart and put a new spirit within you; I will take the heart of stone out of your flesh and give you a heart of flesh. I will put my Spirit within you and cause you to walk in my statutes, and you will keep my judgements and do them' (Ezekiel 36:26-27).

Some people believe that if they just change their ways God's smile will be upon them. They think if they become good citizens, do people good turns, attend church services and mix with good people all will be well with them on judgement day. But this cannot be. They are just the same old sinful people dressed up in new clothes — just as Scuppers was still a dog, no matter what he wore. So it is with humans: a new way of life does not make the person a Christian. 'You must be born again!' said Jesus.

And what you and I cannot do, God does. The new birth is the sovereign work of God's Holy Spirit. If you want to be born again you must pray that God will change your heart. Jesus taught: 'I say to you, ask, and it will be given to you; seek, and you will find; knock, and it will be opened to you... If you then, being evil, know how to give good gifts to your children, how much more will your heavenly Father give the Holy Spirit to those who ask him!' (Luke 11:9-13).

If you sincerely want to become a member of the kingdom of God, then pray that God will send the Holy Spirit into your heart and change you into a new person. But don't pray that prayer unless you are sure you want to become a new person. Paul wrote, 'Therefore, if anyone is in Christ, he is a new creation; old things have passed away; behold, all things have become new' (2 Corinthians 5:17).

You will no longer want to live your old sinful life which you once enjoyed. You may well have to give up old friends who hinder your spiritual life. You will support the work of the church with money, time and energy. You will love your brothers and sisters in Christ. If you are born again your whole way of life will be different. With your new heart you will serve and worship God and you will enjoy doing so.

When you are 'born again' you will be able to repent of your sins, confess them to God and seek his forgiveness. And you will live a holy life because the power of sin in your life will have been broken. No longer will you be a slave to sin (Romans 6:6).

Now ask that important question: 'Have I been born again by the Holy Spirit?' If the answer is, 'Yes', then thank God for his marvellous grace.

If the answer is, 'No' and you want the new birth, then pray that God might show you your sins and your need of a Saviour. If that happens you will run to Christ and find salvation. Our faithful God always keeps his promise (Luke 11:13).

Discuss

1. Nicodemus was involved in three incidents in the New Testament. Today you have read of one; what were the other two incidents? (See John 7:45-52; 19:38-42).
2. What is 'the kingdom of God'?
3. If someone is not a Christian of whose kingdom is he or she a member? (See Ephesians 2:2; Acts 26:18)
4. What must we do to become members of the kingdom of God?

Meditate

Have mercy on me, O God,
   according to your unfailing love;
according to your great compassion
   blot out my transgressions.
Wash away all my iniquity
   and cleanse me from my sin...
Cleanse me with hyssop, and I shall be clean;
   wash me, and I shall be whiter than snow
               (Psalm 51:1-2,7).

Pray

1. Thank God for the wonderful work of the Holy Spirit in making Christians out of rebellious sinners.
2. Pray that each member of your family might come to know Christ as Lord and Saviour.
3. Ask God to blot out all of your sins for the sake of Jesus Christ.
4. Thank God for providing your daily food and other necessities of life.

42. A forgiving God

'If we confess our sins, he is faithful and just to forgive us our sins and to cleanse us from all unrighteousness' (1 John 1:9).

Read Joel 2:12-13

It seems that humans are prone to make mistakes. I am not just speaking about our sins — the breaking of God's law — but in the simple things of life we make errors. I can still remember the spelling mistakes I used to make when there was a word with 'ie' or 'ei' in it. When I found out the rule the problem was overcome.

Even my computer is set up to help me get rid of mistakes. The people who built the computer knew humans would make mistakes when they used their machine. So I find a key with the word 'delete' clearly printed on it. I use it quite a lot. My two-fingered typing makes many errors. On my desk I have a liquid-paper correction pen for the mistakes I make when writing and typing. There is no doubt that the  pencil is a great writing tool, but even pencils have equipment to get rid of writing errors. On the end of my pencil there is a rubber. I find myself using it quite often.

So mistakes are with us all the time. In fact everyone makes mistakes at one time or another. None of us is perfect. Some of the mistakes we make can easily be rubbed out. They don't really matter much to us. But there are mistakes we make which should cause us heartache. These mistakes are called sins and they really matter.

We sin when we break God's law, either by doing something God has forbidden, or by failing to do what he has commanded us to do. Most people think sins are the very wicked things that people do such as murder and robberies. There is no doubt those things are terrible sins, but do you know that not loving God is a terrible sin?

When the Holy Spirit gives a sinner a new heart that person becomes a

Christian. He or she has faith in Christ and loves God. The person also realizes he or she is a sinner who needs forgiveness.

You and I can do nothing to get rid of the stain of our sins. It is not like using the computer, where I highlight my error and then press 'delete'. Sinners must go to God and ask for forgiveness. They must go with a godly sorrow for breaking his law and the intention of not committing that sin again. The Christian hates sin and loves righteousness.

So we go to God in prayer and ask that our sins might be forgiven for the sake of Jesus Christ our Saviour. Our text for today is God's promise to all who truly repent and ask for forgiveness. The apostle John says that we are to confess our sins to God and in return he will forgive us and wash away the terrible stain of sin.

It is wonderful to know that our holy God forgives sinners who seek forgiveness. The very character of God is such that he delights to forgive. God said to the Jewish people through the prophet Joel:

Turn to me with all your heart...
So rend your heart, and not your garments;
Return to the LORD your God,
For he is gracious and merciful,
Slow to anger, and of great kindness...

(Joel 2:12-13).

Our God is a God of mercy who for the sake of his beloved Son removes the stain of sin. Just as 'delete' gets rid of my computer errors, so God takes away the sins of his repentant people.

David the psalmist wrote, 'As far as the east is from the west, so far has he removed our transgressions from us' (Psalm 103:12). That means they are gone for ever because east and west have no fixed point as do north and south. Our sins are gone.

What a wonderful God we have! Micah describes our God as the one who 'delights in mercy'. He writes that God will 'have compassion on us' and 'will cast all our sins into the depths of the sea' (Micah 7:18,19).

In God's sight the sins of his people cannot be seen. He sees Christians as spotless saints, because we are covered with the purity of our Saviour the Lord Jesus Christ. In God's sight we are as pure as our Saviour. This is a glorious truth for which the saints will always praise their God.

Isaiah put it like this:

'Come now, and let us reason together,'
Says the LORD,
'Though your sins are like scarlet,
They shall be as white as snow;

Though they are red like crimson,
They shall be as wool'

(Isaiah 1:18).

Reader, have you truly repented of your sins and confessed them to God, seeking his forgiveness? If so, then you are a citizen of heaven and God is your Father. May this be so with all who read this book.

Discuss

1. Discuss the character of God — his love, mercy, grace, holiness, wisdom and justice.
2. Who was the small man who repented of his sins? What did his repentance involve? (See Luke 19:1-10 and notice especially v.8).
3. Why does God forgive sinners?

Meditate

Remember, O LORD, your great mercy and love,
    for they are from of old.
Remember not the sins of my youth
    and my rebellious ways;
according to your love remember me,
    for you are good, O LORD

(Psalm 25:6-7).

Pray

1. Confess your sins quietly to God and ask for forgiveness.
2. Ask God to help you obey his commands.
3. Ask God to help you to forgive other people when they hurt you.
4. Thank God for his goodness to you and your family.

43. A bottle full of tears

'Put my tears into your bottle...' (Psalm 56:8).

Read Luke 7:36-50

A bottle full of tears? I have a bottle full of old coins as well as another one full of badges and bits and pieces I have saved over the years. My brother John had a bottle full of gold — or almost full of gold — before he sold it. But who would bother to keep their tears in a bottle?

I'm sure everyone reading these words has shed many tears. Sometimes people cry when they are happy, but most tears are caused when people are sad, perhaps at parting from a dear friend, or because they are sorry for something they have done, or because they have been hurt. We have caused hurt to someone else and that person has shed tears. Others have hurt us and our tears have fallen. Can you remember any tears you have shed because you were happy? Are you able to remember tears that you have shed because of unhappy situations?

David had suffered terribly at the hands of King Saul and as a result had shed many tears. David had also committed great sins. When he repented he did so with many tears. God had been offended by David's sin and this upset David greatly. David had seen the death of many who were dear to him and then too the tears had flowed.

David wanted God to remember the times when his tears had flowed, for his tears were a sign of deep sorrow for sins. Other tears had flowed because of the hurt others caused him. Maybe David kept a bottle in which he caught his tears. This bottle of tears would be evidence of his repentance and of the sorrow others had caused him. David had evidence to present to God of his true sorrow.

In today's reading we have the wonderful story of a sinful woman who came to Jesus while he was eating at the home of an important Pharisee. This woman had seen how her sins offended God. She was truly repentant of all that she had done. Luke tells us that this woman bowed down before Jesus and wept tears over his feet. In fact Jesus said of the woman, 'She has washed my feet with her tears...' (v. 44). I often wonder if this poor, sinful, but repentant woman had a bottle full of tears. Maybe she kept a precious bottle of tears of repentance and now used them to wash the feet of the one person who could forgive her all of her sins.

The woman then wiped Jesus' feet with her hair. She also rubbed a precious, sweet-smelling oil onto Christ's feet. Then she kissed the Saviour's feet. Why did she do this?

Jesus said to the people who saw what was happening, 'Therefore I say to you, her sins, which are many, are forgiven, for she loved much. But to whom little is forgiven, the same loves little' (v. 47). The woman was a great sinner who repented of her sins. She showed her repentance and love for Christ by her actions. Because her many sins were forgiven, her love for Christ was great.

That repentant woman finally heard the words from Christ which she really wanted to hear: 'Your sins are forgiven... Your faith has saved you. Go in peace' (vv. 48,50).

Reader, have you seen your sins? Have you gone to Jesus and asked for forgiveness, maybe with tears falling from your eyes because you have offended God? If so then your love for Christ should be great because God has forgiven your sins for the sake of his beloved Son. You don't need to keep a bottle of tears as evidence of the tears you have shed. God knows the thoughts of your heart. He understands all your feelings. He knows if your tears are genuine or not. All is recorded in God's book of remembrance.

On judgement day the books will be opened and all will be revealed. How will you be on that day?

Discuss

1. Why do people cry?
2. List two instances when Jesus shed tears. Why was he weeping? (Luke 19:41; John 11:35).
3. Who washed the Lord's feet with tears?
4. What does it mean to repent?

Meditate

All my enemies whisper together against me;
   they imagine the worst for me, saying,
'A vile disease has beset him;
   he will never get up from the place where he
      lies.'
Even my close friend, whom I trusted,
   he who shared my bread,
      has lifted up his heel against me.
But you, O LORD, have mercy on me...
                              (Psalm 41:7-10).

Pray

1. Ask God to give you a true understanding of the wickedness of sin.
2. Pray that God will make you truly repentant of your sins.
3. Thank God for the wonderful Saviour of sinners, the Lord Jesus Christ.
4. Pray that the Holy Spirit might give you a heart of compassion for everyone you know.

44.   An angel of light?

'And no wonder! For Satan himself transforms himself into an angel of light' (2 Corinthians 11:14).

Read 2 Thessalonians 2:1-12

When I attended teachers' college all the members of the class were given an assignment. It was very simple but took some research. We each had to discover thirty words in common use which could not be found in the dictionary. I found this quite easy, as I took the newspaper and looked through the pages and pages of advertisements. I soon found thirty new words.

Today the same is happening: new words are finding their way into our vocabulary — words I have never before heard. One such word is 'morphing'. Some time ago I was watching TV when I saw an advertisement for a new car. It was a good-looking, red sports car. It was being driven along a country road at a very fast pace. Then before my eyes the car was transformed into a leopard running along the same country road.

I had seen this happen on TV before, and on that earlier occasion it was easy to see the stages in the changes, but not this time. The car very smoothly turned into a leopard. I was amazed and eventually taped the advertisement and played it through many times trying to see the stages of the change. But it all happened so smoothly that I was amazed. Now, of course, we can buy a programme for our computers and do the same. This amazing technology is called 'morphing'.

Our text tells us that Satan is involved in the activity of 'morphing'. Yes, that wicked one, who has brought sin and death into this world, is able to transform himself into an angel of light.

While we don't see Satan walking about, he and his demons are there, tempting people to sin. If Satan appeared to you and said, 'I am Satan. I want you to deliberately disobey all of God's commands,' I am sure you would recognize him for what he is — the enemy of God and Christ. However, Satan does not do that. He uses people to lead others away from God and his truth.

Our Bible passage for the day calls one of Satan's followers 'the man of sin' (v. 3). Of course, Satan has many such followers. Only a very few stand up and say to the world, 'I'm a follower of Satan. Follow me!' No, they pretend to be what they are not. They pretend to be lovable people who want the best for everyone.

Paul says that these people are quite capable of doing powerful works. Why, they can even perform miracles! Jesus spoke of them when he said that on judgement day they would cry out, 'Lord, Lord, have we not prophesied in your name, cast out demons in your name, and done many wonders in your name?' (Matthew 7:22).

If a person turned up in town claiming to cast out demons in Christ's name I'm sure many people would say, 'Here's a man of God!' Then if it appeared that he and his followers healed a few sick people, many would flock to their meetings. But how are people to know if these miracle-workers come from God or are deluded followers of Satan? Do you remember our text, Paul's words of warning: 'Satan himself transforms himself into an angel of light'?

Satan's representatives are able to appear as angels of light — spokesmen of God. They encourage people to follow their teaching and so lead many along a pathway to hell. Of course, the pathway they walk is often enjoyable and this is what people love.

The church takes the place of the club. It is all so exciting, seeing people falling over and laughing. Then others are throwing away their crutches and walking. Often there is a good band playing popular tunes as well as plenty of singing. Yes, people love this type of activity. But what about the teaching in the sermon? So often it is just lies, or lies mixed with a little truth. Yes, Satan can transform himself into an angel of light and people love his lies.

God gives all who love and follow Satan's lies a severe warning: 'And for this reason God will send them strong delusion, that they should believe the lie, that they all may be condemned who did not believe the truth but had pleasure in unrighteousness' (2 Thessalonians 2:11-12). On judgement day Christ will say to all who follow Satan's human teachers, 'I never knew you; depart from me, you who practise lawlessness' (Matthew 7:23).

How, then, do you know who is a minister of Christ and who is a minister of Satan, the evil one? The answer is quite simple: is this person teaching the truth as it is found in the Scriptures? This means you must be students of the Scriptures, knowing the doctrines of Christ.

Do you remember when Paul and Silas went to preach the gospel to the Bereans? The Bereans listened carefully to what was taught, but then went home to search the Scriptures to make sure what they heard was God's truth. This is the way you will ensure that you are not lead astray by Satan and his human henchmen who appear as angels of light. Satan's followers are very good at 'morphing'. So open your Bible, read and study and live out God's commands.

Discuss

1. Who was Satan before he sinned? (Read Isaiah 14:12-15 and discuss).
2. Why do you think Satan hates God?
3. Read 2 Timothy 2:14-17 and discuss the teaching contained in it.

Meditate

Answer me when I call to you,
    O my righteous God.
Give me relief from my distress;
    be merciful to me and hear my prayer.
How long, O men, will you turn my glory into
    shame?
How long will you love delusions and seek false
    gods?
Know that the LORD has set apart the godly for
    himself;
    the LORD will hear when I call to him
                        (Psalm 4:1-3).

Pray

1. Thank God for giving you faithful teachers of spiritual truth.
2. Thank God for the Scriptures and your ability to read them.
3. Pray that God will keep you safe from those who would lead you away from his truth.

45. God in flesh and blood

'But when the fulness of time had come, God sent forth his Son, born of a woman, born under the law, to redeem those who were under the law, that we might receive the adoption as sons' (Galatians 4:4-5).

Read Philippians 2:5-11

There are important people we know who always seem distant from us. They mix with other important people and always seem to be dressed in the best of clothes. Their photographs appear in the newspapers, they are well-spoken, their hair is always in place and their clothes are spotless.

At one school where I taught one of the parents was such a man. He was very wealthy, owning a very profitable business. He employed many men and women and was looked up to by the community as a well-to-do man. I had spoken to him on occasions and found him to be a very pleasant person.

A working-day was called for the parents of the schoolchildren, as the playground needed brightening up. I had met most of the parents and thought I knew who would be present to help with the work. I didn't expect that important, well-to-do man to be there. He just didn't seem to be the type to get involved with the other parents in hard, dirty work. But I was wrong. He was there in his old working-clothes. His sleeves were rolled up and he was ready for work. And he worked all day.

He went home tired and dirty. He had worked hard and the men who worked with him appreciated what he had done.

In a small way he reminds me of the Lord Jesus Christ coming into this world. Christ is Jehovah. He is the Son of the Father. In the eternity before he came into this world he existed with the Father and the Holy Spirit

— one God, yet three distinct persons. The three persons in the Godhead didn't need a creation to be perfectly content. We have no real idea of the glory and wonder that existed in the Godhead. The angels in heaven bowed before God in adoration and wonder and praised their Creator and Sustainer.

You all know the story of creation and how sin entered through the rebellion of Satan and then his temptation of Adam and Eve. God's plan to save sinful men and women meant that Christ had to enter the world of sin. He had to become a man so he could represent his people. This truth is found prophesied again and again in the Old Testament. Isaiah wrote, 'Behold, the virgin shall conceive and bear a Son, and shall call his name Immanuel' (Isaiah 7:14). And the name Immanuel means 'God with us'!

Christ had to live in perfect obedience to God his Father. He also had to bear the punishment of God due to his people for their sins.

So Christ entered this world, being born as a baby to a virgin. He was willing to step down from the throne of heaven and take a body of flesh and blood so that he could save his people.

Jesus in many ways had a body like ours. He felt pain and his body became tired. He shed tears and, even though we are not told about it, I'm sure he must have smiled and laughed like other people. He wore clothes and at times would have had dirt and dust on his body. As a baby he drank milk from his mother Mary's breast. He played with other children and probably stubbed his toe and hurt himself just like you and I have done.

But there was a big difference between Jesus and all other humans: he was born without sin and at no time did he sin. He could not sin, because Jesus Christ is both God and man in the one person — and God can't sin!

Just as that man I told you about took off his splendid clothes and joined in with the other workers, so Christ left the glory of heaven and lived amongst men and women. When people saw Jesus walking down the street with dusty feet, dirty clothes, looking very tired and with perspiration on his face I'm sure they didn't say, 'Look, there is God!' Our passage of Scripture tells us that Christ humbled himself and came into the world looking like a human, because he was human.

He was whipped and blood flowed from the wounds in his back. Jesus felt the pain and saw the blood on his body. He was treated terribly by those wicked people and eventually was nailed to the cross. He felt the pain of the nails tearing through his flesh. He saw his precious blood dripping onto the ground below his body. He heard the people calling out for him to be crucified. He felt the pain of it all. On the cross we are told that he was thirsty. He knew that Satan was tormenting him. Finally, he died and his body was placed in a tomb.

The God-man, Jesus Christ, lived and died so that sinners might be saved. Reader, consider what Christ has done for you. If you are a Christian thank him for leaving heaven and coming to this earth and saving you. He suffered so that you might be saved. The writer to the Hebrews penned these wonderful words: 'But we see Jesus, who was made a little lower than the angels, for the suffering of death crowned with glory and honour, that he, by the grace of God, might taste death for everyone' (Hebrews 2:9). In that body he suffered for you and me.

Let us always praise God for the work of salvation that is found in Jesus Christ. Christ left his place of perfection and glory and came into our sinful world to save his people. This he did through his perfect life and death. What a debt of gratitude we owe our Saviour!

Discuss

1. Why did Christ visit earth some two thousand years ago? (Read and discuss 1 Timothy 1:14-17).
2. Why did Christ become a man?
3. Was it possible for Christ to commit sin? Why?

Meditate

Sacrifice and offering you did not desire,
    but my ears you have pierced;
burnt offerings and sin offerings
    you did not require.
Then I said, 'Here am I, I have come—
    it is written about me in the scroll.
I desire to do your will, O my God;
    your law is within my heart.'

(Psalm 40:6-8).

Pray

1. Thank Christ for coming to earth to die for sinners.
2. Pray that God will give you a deeper understanding of the person of the Lord Jesus Christ.
3. Pray for the day when you will meet Jesus Christ face to face.

46. Everything is ready for you

'Then one of the seven angels ...
came to me and talked with me,
saying, "Come I will show you
the bride, the Lamb's wife"'
(Revelation 21:9).

Read Revelation 21:9-21

It is wise to have things ready for use when you need them. It can be a wonderful surprise if someone else has done the work for you. Sometimes, just before she starts getting dinner ready Valerie says, 'Wouldn't it be wonderful to find the table set and the food waiting to be eaten?' I'm sure there are times when you wish that someone else made your bed while you were getting washed and dressed.

When Val and I were married we had no home of our own. At that stage of our life we didn't have enough money to buy or build a home. In fact we lived in a hotel for two weeks after we returned from our honeymoon. We had to search for a home to rent. As schoolteachers we were both appointed to schools in a large city. One of our friends didn't have to worry about working to buy a home. A relative died and when our friend married, the home was there waiting for him and his new wife.

The Bible tells us that Jesus Christ has gone to heaven and is now preparing 'dwelling-places' for his people. This is a wonderful truth. In the Old Testament we find that God prepared a place on the earth for his chosen people, Israel.

When God was ready to bring his people out of Egypt and set them free, he had no intention of letting them wander about for ever without a home to call their own. We read, 'So I have come down to deliver them out of the hand of the Egyptians, and to bring them up from that land to a good and large land, to a land flowing with milk and honey...' (Exodus 3:8).

When the Israelites fought their way, with God's help, into Canaan, they found themselves in a land that was just what they needed. Our ancestors had to clear the land, build homes and plant their crops. But the Israelites found their new land was ready for them. Homes were everywhere. Cities had been built and crops were growing. Under their great leader Joshua the land was divided between the tribes and very quickly the people settled down into their God-given country.

But we must remember that to get to that wonderful land, the nation of Israel wandered through the wilderness. They lived in tents and depended upon God to supply their needs. They truly were pilgrims in a harsh wilderness.

Today Christians are like those wandering Israelites of old — we too are pilgrims. The writer to the Hebrews said of all the saints in the Old Testament: 'These all died in faith, not having received the promises, but having seen them afar off were assured of them, embraced them, and confessed that they were strangers and pilgrims on the earth. For those who say such things declare plainly that they seek a homeland... But now they desire a better, that is, a heavenly country. Therefore God is not ashamed to be called their God, for he has prepared a city for them' (Hebrews 11:13-16). This earth is not our true home. Many times we find life very difficult. We depend upon God for help when the going gets really tough. And as God helped the Israelites of old, so he continually comes to our aid.

What about God's people today? I can't prepare a home to use when I die. But, praise God, my Lord Jesus Christ has gone on ahead to prepare those dwelling-places the saints will one day need. New, perfect bodies will also be ready for us on the resurrection day. Our souls will not be naked.

Christ has told us that he has prepared a home for each one of his people. When he returns, he will do so in all of his power and glory. This great event will bring the history of this world to an end and eternity will commence for everyone.

On that day God will remake this creation. There will be new heavens and a new earth. This old world of sin, trouble and death will be gone for ever — burned up. Then the new Jerusalem will descend from heaven to the new earth. What a wonderful city that new Jerusalem is! You have read the description of it in today's reading. Everything will then be perfect. The saints will not have to build homes for themselves. They will not have to work for years to earn money to buy new houses. Christ has done it all for them. The saints will simply move into their new homes.

But that new Jerusalem described by the angel is not just a city; it is the bride of Christ. This is really a description of all who believe in Jesus Christ for salvation. We shall, by God's grace, be a glorious people.

Soon, brothers and sisters in Christ, our pilgrimage in this world will come to an end. We shall go to be with our Lord Jesus Christ. Then we shall return with him to live in the wonderful paradise he has prepared for us. May we all have a longing in our hearts for that great day.

Discuss

1. Take out an atlas and find Egypt and Israel. Talk together about the journey of God's people as they found their way to the promised land.
2. Why do you think the walls of the city were built on the foundation of the apostles?
3. Why were the gates to the city named after the twelve tribes of Israel?
4. Who will have a part in that great city?
5. In heaven, what is the home for the soul? (See 2 Corinthians 5:1-8).

Meditate

You will arise and have compassion on Zion,
    for it is time to show favour to her;
    the appointed time has come.
For her stones are dear to your servants;
    her very dust moves them to pity.
The nations will fear the name of the LORD,
    all the kings of the earth will revere your glory.
For the LORD will rebuild Zion
    and appear in his glory
                                        (Psalm 102:13-16).

Pray

1. Thank God for giving your family a home in which to live.
2. Thank God for the Scriptures that tell his people the way of salvation and about the glory that awaits them.
3. Thank God for giving you people who are concerned about your relationship with Jesus Christ, people who teach you of Christ and who pray for you.
4. Ask God to make you a faithful Christian.

47. Welcome into paradise

'And Jesus said to him, "Assuredly, I say to you, today you will be with me in Paradise"' (Luke 23:43).

Read Revelation 2:1-7

A poor thief, hanging on a cross beside the Lord Jesus Christ, asked that he be remembered when Christ came into his kingdom. This thief had not been a church-goer. He had not been baptized. He had never sat at the Lord's table. In fact till that time at the very end of his life, people probably thought him to be a wicked man, with no hope when he met God on judgement day.

But, hanging on the cross, he realized that Jesus Christ was a king and would soon be sitting upon his throne. He repented of his sins and believed what he had heard about Christ. Then looking towards Christ he made a simple request: 'Lord, remember me when you come into your kingdom' (Luke 23:42). What a wonderful reply he heard! Christ promised him that they would be together in paradise.

What is paradise and what picture does this give us of heaven? 'Paradise' is an old Persian word meaning a walled garden. The Persian kings built the most beautiful gardens. Usually these gardens had streams flowing through them. Shrubs, trees and flowers would be found everywhere. Plenty of fruit trees and vines with the sweetest of fruit would be found. Visitors would be able to reach out and take what they wanted to eat.

I'm sure these gardens would have been lovely cool

places in that hot part of the world. Each home-owner would have his small garden and there in the cool the family would entertain visitors.

Sometimes one of the Persian kings would reward those in the kingdom who did well with an invitation to walk in his garden. These visitors walked with the king in paradise. They enjoyed the friendship of the others in the garden, eating together and talking, not only with one another, but also with the king.

The Garden of Eden was a paradise. Streams flowed through that garden where every tree, shrub, flower and grass grew in abundance. There Adam and Eve lived in peace with each other and the animals. They were to look after God's garden. But the greatest blessing of all was that in paradise they walked and talked with God, the King of creation (Genesis 3:8).

Today's reading is about the church at Ephesus. Once this was a loving, faithful church, but now things had changed. Many of the children and grandchildren, as well as some of the newcomers to the church, had no real love for Christ. The church still did some good works, but not because of love for Christ. I think the church had become an enjoyable club for its members.

The King of the church, the Lord Jesus Christ, called upon the members of that church to repent of their sins and fall in love with him once again. If they did, then great things were in store for those repentant church members. We read, 'To him who overcomes I will give to eat from the tree of life, which is in the midst of the Paradise of God' (Revelation 2:7).

This wonderful paradise will be our dwelling-place for ever. In that garden we shall find a river flowing with the 'water of life' (Revelation 22:1-2,17). We shall be able to drink from that river whenever we like. 'The tree of life' will also be found there.

In God's paradise we shall mix with all the saints but, best of all, we shall see the King of paradise. Isaiah tells us, 'Your eyes will see the King in his beauty; they will see the land that is very far off' (Isaiah 33:17). We shall see our Saviour's face (Revelation 22:4).

There will be peace in God's paradise. There are two passages of Scripture that I love for they speak of the tranquillity of heaven. First we read:

They shall beat their swords into ploughshares,
And their spears into pruning hooks;
Nation shall not lift up sword against nation,
Neither shall they learn war any more.
But everyone shall sit under his vine and under his fig tree,
And no one shall make them afraid

(Micah 4:3-4).

Then we find:

> The wolf also shall dwell with the lamb,
> The leopard shall lie down with the young goat,
> The calf and the young lion and the fatling together;
> And a little child shall lead them.
> The cow and the bear shall graze;
> Their young ones shall lie down together;
> And the lion shall eat straw like the ox.
> The nursing child shall play by the cobra's hole,
> And the weaned child shall put his hand in the viper's den.
> They shall not hurt nor destroy in all my holy mountain,
> For the earth shall be full of the knowledge of the LORD
> As the waters cover the sea
>
> (Isaiah 11:6-9).

It all sounds glorious, but remember what Paul said:

> Eye has not seen, nor ear heard,
> Nor have entered into the heart of man
> The things which God has prepared for those who love him
>
> (1 Corinthians 2:9).

The most important question for you to think about is: 'Will I one day live in God's paradise?'

Discuss

1. Discuss the passage quoted from Isaiah 11:6-9. Why do you think the lion will eat straw and not some other animal's flesh?
2. What do you think will be the best thing about paradise?
3. There will be peace in paradise. What is this 'peace'?
4. What is meant in the Bible by the word 'church'?
5. What was spiritually wrong with the church at Ephesus?

Meditate

The LORD is my shepherd, I shall not be in want.
    He makes me lie down in green pastures,
he leads me beside quiet waters,
    he restores my soul.
He guides me in paths of righteousness
    for his name's sake

(Psalm 23:1-3).

Pray

1. Give thanks to God for the paradise his people will inherit.
2. Ask the Lord to forgive your sins and help you live a holy life.
3. Ask God to give you and all members of your family a true love for worship on the Lord's Day.

48. Paradise — a place of holiness

'Nevertheless we, according to his promise, look for new heavens and a new earth in which righteousness dwells' (2 Peter 3:13).

| **Read** Revelation 21:22-27 |

The great longing of God's people here on earth is that they might be holy. This means they do not want to be like the ungodly people of this world, but like Jesus — 'conformed to the image of his [God's] Son' (Romans 8:29).

The psalmist puts it this way: 'As for me, I will see your face in righteousness; I shall be satisfied when I awake in your likeness' (Psalm 17:15). And this is the desire of all of God's people — to be like him, perfect in holiness.

Paradise is the land of holiness, because it is the dwelling-place of God. We read in Psalm 33:13-14: 'The LORD looks from heaven ... from the place of his habitation.' His dwelling-place is the place of perfection!

We are able to build lovely gardens around our houses, but they never seem to stay that way. We have a nice front garden with brightly-coloured flowers everywhere, but every now and again a dog gets in and does damage. Once I went to a lot of trouble growing tulips. They were just flowering when one night two dogs found their way into the garden. I woke up to hear them fighting. By the time I arrived on the scene my tulips were destroyed.

When I was young I remember cows breaking through the fence and into the garden of our house. That garden was important to Mum and Dad. There they grew what was needed for food on the table. I can remember a big mulberry tree in one corner. (I drove past the farm a couple of years ago — the house and sheds were gone, but the mulberry tree was still there.) The cows broke through the fence to eat the green vegetables that grew in abundance. The fence had to be repaired, but the cows broke it down a second time. Dad then really went to work and the new fence stopped the cows from breaking through.

God's paradise is the dwelling-place of the saints — the holy ones. Think seriously about these words describing heaven: 'And God will wipe away every tear from their eyes; there shall be no more death, nor sorrow, nor crying; and there shall be no more pain, for the former things have passed away' (Revelation 21:4). Heaven sounds a wonderful place. Everything that causes unhappiness will be gone for ever. There will be no more tears and aches and sorrows, no more parting from loved ones because of death.

Why? The answer is so simple: the cause of all our troubles is gone for ever. In paradise there is no sin! Just think of it! There is no evil in God's dwelling-place, no Satan to tempt the saints to sin, because he and his followers have been confined to everlasting hell.

But is it possible for sin to raise its head in God's paradise? The cows might have broken into the garden at home, but sinners cannot enter God's paradise. The Persian kings had good strong walls around their gardens to keep out everything that could upset the peace of the place. Our reading tells us that the new Jerusalem, God's paradise, will have a wall about it. This will prevent everything that is evil from entering. The gates in the wall are open to the saints, but outside the wall 'are dogs and sorcerers and sexually immoral and murderers and idolaters, and whoever loves and practises a lie' (Revelation 22:15).

What shall we be like when we enter paradise? The apostle John says, 'It has not yet been revealed what we shall be, but we know that when he is revealed, we shall be like him, for we shall see him as he is' (1 John 3:2). We shall be like him! We shall be perfect in holiness — clothed in Christ's righteousness. We shall love that holy place because we shall be holy and love all that is holy and good. At last we shall be at home — no longer pilgrims walking the sinful earth, but residents of heaven, paradise prepared by Christ for his people.

Someone once said that God's paradise is 'a prepared place for a prepared people'. Are you being prepared for that heavenly home? Will you receive that crown of righteousness?

Discuss

1. What is meant by 'holiness'?
2. God has told us that without holiness we can never enter heaven (Hebrews 12:14). We are not holy people. How then can we ever hope to enter heaven?
3. We are told that Jesus came to save us from our sins (Matthew 1:21). What does this mean?

Meditate

Your statutes are wonderful;
　　therefore I obey them.
The unfolding of your words gives light;
　　it gives understanding to the simple.
I open my mouth and pant,
　　longing for your commands
(Psalm 119:129-131).

Pray

1. Ask God to give you a real love for his Word.
2. Thank God for his perfect law and ask the Holy Spirit to guide you in the pathways of righteousness.
3. Ask God to make you a gentle and loving Christian.
4. Thank God for forgiving all of your sins.

49. Oh, to see her face!

'As for me, I will see your face in righteousness; I shall be satisfied when I awake in your likeness' (Psalm 17:15).

Read Revelation 22:1-5

Most people enjoy looking at the face of someone they love. We love being near that person and don't like being away from him or her for any great length of time. I often think of the soldiers in wartime who were away from their loved ones for years. How husbands and wives must have missed each other! And I'm sure children missed parents who were absent on war duty. The truth is that we want to be with those we love.

Think of the babies born just a few months after fathers left for the battlefield. For years they were without Dad being with them. But I'm sure their mothers told them about the man who was their father. Many times a lonely mother would have taken out a photograph of Dad and proudly showed it to her children. When letters arrived they would have been read, and probably some tears would have fallen from Mum's eyes. There would have been that great longing for the family to be together again — to be able to look at each other and hold one another close.

When Valerie and I were courting we taught at schools hundreds of miles apart. We only saw each other every three months when school holidays arrived. But we wrote to each other. Sometimes we used the telephone to speak to each other. Of course we had photographs and that was good. But more than anything else we longed to see each other face to face and be with one other.

Today's text was written by David, a man who loved God. He knew about God. He had much of the Old Testament to read. This was to him a letter from the God he loved. God had spoken to David and made great promises to him. God even sent the prophet Nathan to him.

David loved God with all his heart and soul. But just reading about God and speaking to him in prayer was not enough. He longed to see God. But no one can see God, because he is spirit. The one David longed to see was the Lord Jesus Christ, God's only begotten Son.

But when Christ visited this earth only a very few people showed a saving interest in him. There seemed to be nothing very special about him. Isaiah had this to say about Jesus Christ:

He has no form or comeliness;
And when we see him,
There is no beauty that we should desire him.
He is despised and rejected by men...

(Isaiah 53:2-3).

But all who loved him, and all who have loved him since he walked the streets of Jerusalem, long to see him. John wrote these words about all who are saved by the work of Christ: 'Beloved, now we are children of God; and it has not yet been revealed what we shall be, but we know that when he is revealed, we shall be like him, for we shall see him as he is' (1 John 3:2).

This will be the most wonderful event in our love for Jesus Christ. We shall see, face to face, the one who loved us and gave himself for us. He also will see us face to face. The apostle John wrote of that wonderful day: 'Behold, the tabernacle of God is with men, and he will dwell with them, and they shall be his people. God himself will be with them and be their God' (Revelation 21:3).

Do you remember our text for this chapter? David longed for the day when he would see God. We should all be longing for that day when we shall gaze upon the face of our beloved Saviour — the one we love and the one who first loved us.

We shall no longer need to read about Jesus, or to bow down in secret and pray to the one we love, but cannot see. In heaven we shall see him face to face. Then we shall truly be like him. We shall have his righteousness given to us as new clothing. Sin will be gone for ever. We shall love righteousness. What a wonderful day! Are you ready for that day?

Discuss

1. Why do most family members like being at home with their family?
2. Who is your spiritual father? Who is the father of unbelievers?
3. Who was Nathan? (Read 1 Kings 1:8 and 2 Samuel 12:1-14 and discuss).
4. The Bible tells us that one day we shall be like Christ. What effect should this have on our lives now? (See 1 John 3:2-3).

Meditate

The Mighty One, God, the LORD,
    speaks and summons the earth
    from the rising of the sun to the place where
        it sets...
Our God comes and will not be silent...
He summons the heavens above,
    and the earth, that he may judge his people:
'Gather to me my consecrated ones...'

(Psalm 50:1-5).

Pray

1. Pray that God might give you a true joy as you worship and serve him.
2. Ask God to give you a true hunger and thirst after righteousness.
3. Ask God to give you a longing to meet Jesus.

50. A great feast

"'Let us be glad and rejoice and give him glory, for the marriage of the Lamb has come, and his wife has made herself ready." And to her it was granted to be arrayed in fine linen, clean and bright, for the fine linen is the righteous acts of the saints. Then he said to me, "Write: 'Blessed are those who are called to the marriage supper of the Lamb!'"
(Revelation 19:7-9).

Read Matthew 22:1-14

In our modern world, meals are not the enjoyable experiences they once were. Everyone is in a hurry. When I was young, Mum spent a lot of time in the kitchen preparing meals. I can still remember the stove we kept stoking with wood. There was always a kettle of water boiling, ready for making a pot of tea. And there was always the smell of food cooking in the oven.

When we had our meals we all sat down, and after thanking the Lord for providing us with our daily food we ate together. We spent time talking and laughing. Sometimes we would have to hurry, but mostly we took our time

eating and enjoying our food. If we had visitors Mum would go to more trouble making sure things were just right. And we would then linger a little longer around the table. Eating was an enjoyable time of friendship where we shared the day's events with each other.

Things are a bit different today in most homes. So often it is Kentucky Fried or Macdonalds, or some other takeaway food. I've also seen people eating their meal in the car as they drove along. In so many homes meals are eaten on laps while watching the TV. Everything is over and done with so quickly. There is no real pleasure and friendship in eating any more. We live in a world where so many homes are like hotels — places to sleep after a day of rushing about.

When God was about to bring his people out of the land of slavery, Egypt, he told them to have a meal and to eat it in haste. A lamb was to be roasted and eaten on the night when the angel would kill the first-born of all who had not marked their doorposts and lintels with the blood of the lamb. God, through Moses, told the people to be ready to leave Egypt at a moment's notice 'with a belt on your waist, your sandals on your feet, and your staff in your hand. So you shall eat it in haste' (Exodus 12:11).

But when the Israelites celebrated the Passover each year the family ate their meal as a celebration where God was thanked for his goodness to his people. The Jewish family sat about the table enjoying their meal together. There was no need to eat in haste.

Today we have the Lord's Supper, which is a simple meal signifying the saving work of the Lord Jesus. This meal of bread and wine is a reminder to us all that Christ died for his people — that his blood was shed and his body broken for his people. The Lord's Supper also reminds us that Christ will come again to gather his people to himself.

Christians have meals together — meals where they take their time and talk to each other about things that happen in their lives and there is also time to talk about God's great blessings in Christ.

Meals speak of love and friendship. Today's reading is about a wedding feast that the king prepared for his guests. It was to be a wonderful time, for the king's son was to be married. The guests had been invited and now the servants were sent out to remind them of the important day. Many of those invited made excuses why they could not come to the wedding. But the king filled up the palace dining room with all who would come. Each person was given a special garment to wear. It was a wonderful time of friendship, love and a leisurely eaten meal in the presence of the king, his son and the bride and all the other guests.

Of course, we know that this parable spoke about the Jews who were invited to follow Christ for salvation. But the nation of Israel wanted nothing to do with Jesus Christ. They crucified him. As a result the gospel was taken to the Gentiles. Many of the Gentiles heard the good news of Jesus

Christ and entered the kingdom of God. They, with the believing Jews, would one day sit down with the king and enjoy the festivities he had prepared for them. After all, the saints are not just guests, but they are the bride of the King's Son — Jesus Christ. The angels of God will gather Christ's people together and take them to be with their Bridegroom, Jesus Christ.

Today's text speaks of this great feast that God has prepared for his people — people who love, serve and worship the Son of God. We have special clothing to wear. We are all clothed in the righteousness of Christ. Our text also tells us that our acts of obedience are a part of our clothing as well.

John the apostle heard a voice from heaven which said, "'Blessed are the dead who die in the Lord from now on.' 'Yes,' says the Spirit, 'that they may rest from their labours, and their works follow them'" (Revelation 14:13). Our imperfect works have been made good by the perfect righteousness of Christ. Our clothing is that which comes from the righteousness of Christ.

And together the saints will sit down at the wedding breakfast, in the presence of God, with Jesus Christ at the head of the table and there they will praise and glorify the Saviour. We shall enjoy his presence. We shall talk about the wonder of our salvation and together thank God for what he has done for us.

The picture we have in today's text is one of joy that lasts for ever. It is a picture of love for the Lord Jesus Christ and his love for his people. I pray that all my readers have a seat ready and waiting for them at that wedding feast. I trust that you have accepted the King's invitation to come to the feast. I pray you love the King's Son and long to be with him. After all, he is your beloved Bridegroom! May God's blessing be yours today and for ever!

Discuss

1. Christians eat the Lord's Supper together. What is the significance of this meal? (See 1 Corinthians 11:23-26).
2. What difference in meaning is there between the words 'joy' and 'happiness'?
3. Discuss the teachings of the parable you have read today.

Meditate

How can I repay the LORD
    for all his goodness to me?
I will lift up the cup of salvation
    and call on the name of the LORD.
I will fulfil my vows to the LORD
    in the presence of all his people
                         (Psalm 116:12-14).

Pray

1. Thank God for providing you with your daily food and other necessities of life.
2. Thank God for his great love for his people.
3. Pray that God might bless your minister and all who guide you spiritually.
4. Pray that God might bless your schoolteachers.

51.   Locked out!

'Watch therefore, for you know neither the day nor the hour in which the Son of Man is coming' (Matthew 25:13).

Read Matthew 25:1-13

The lesson that is taught in the parable of the ten virgins is that, at every moment of our lives, we must be ready for the return of Jesus Christ.

I have already told you about my little dog called Wags. He is thoroughly spoilt and both Valerie and I love that little bundle of white fluff. We take him for a walk nearly every day. And if we mention a ride in the car he runs to the front door and sits there waiting for the door to be opened so he can run out to the car and jump in. He loves the warm weather but doesn't like the cold of winter.

He usually goes to bed when we do and often he doesn't get up till well after Val and I are out and about. He would never make a good working dog! But some mornings he wakes up and we hear him scratching at the door to go outside. He wants to get out. So one of us has to get up and open the door for him. We leave the door open just enough for him to get back inside. He never stays outside very long on cold, frosty mornings. When he returns he comes into our room and tries to jump up on the foot of our bed.